THE
SHORT
LIFE
OF
SOPHIE
SCHOLL

THE SHORT LIFE OF SOPHIE SCHOLL

Hermann Vinke

WITH AN INTERVIEW WITH ILSE AICHINGER
TRANSLATED FROM THE GERMAN BY HEDWIG PACHTER

Harper & Row, Publishers

Library of Congress Cataloging in Publication Data
Vinke, Hermann.
    The short life of Sophie Scholl.

    Translation of: Das kurze Leben der Sophie Scholl.
    Summary: The biography of the twenty-one-year-old
German student who was put to death for her anti-Nazi
activities with the underground group called the White
Rose.
    1. Scholl, Sophie, 1921–1943. 2. Weisse Rose (Resist-
ance group) 3. Anti-Nazi movement—Biography. 4. Uni-
versität München—Riot, 1943. [1. Scholl, Sophie, 1921–
1943. 2. White Rose (Resistance group) 3. Anti-Nazi
movement—Biography. 4. World War, 1939–1945—Underground movements—Germany] I. Aichinger, Ilse.
II. Title.
DD256.3.S337V5613 1984   943.086'0924 [B] [92]   82-47714
ISBN 0-06-026302-4
ISBN 0-06-026303-2 (lib. bdg.)

Contents

Photographs and Drawings
from the Scholl family collection

INTRODUCTION: *A Book on Sophie Scholl?*

Is it possible to write a book just on Sophie Scholl? Don't the brother and sister, Hans and Sophie Scholl, belong together? Some people posed that question when I started to work on this book in the summer of 1979. There was no easy answer at first. After all, Sophie Scholl did grow up with her brother. She loved him as only a brother can be loved. She studied with him in Munich, and she joined the resistance group he had founded, the White Rose. Together, they fought the Nazi dictatorship with leaflets from the underground, and together, in February 1943, they paid the price for their resistance with their lives.

Yet there is good reason for a book on Sophie Scholl. Despite her fondness for her brother Hans, she was quite an independent person. Even as a young girl she had a singular way of holding her own, thinking her own thoughts, doing her own things. We can see this in her numerous letters and diary notes, some of which appear in this book. Whether they describe nature or her own life, they are bound to pull the reader into the depth of her involvement. To my surprise, I myself came to feel a brotherly affection for her and to speak of her familiarly.

In this book, Inge Aicher-Scholl—she and her sister

1

Elisabeth are the only survivors of the five children—tells of important phases in Sophie's life. As the oldest of Mayor Robert Scholl's children, she witnessed Hans and Sophie's ordeal at close hand and suffered with them. Their youngest brother, Werner, died at the Russian front during World War II. For the past ten years she and her husband, the graphic designer Otl Aicher, have been living in the Rotismühle, once a dilapidated grain- and sawmill, now rebuilt by Otl Aicher and surrounded by some graphically designed buildings. Set in the lovely southern German countryside, it is far from noisy city streets and factories.

It is in the Rotismühle that I talked with Inge about Sophie Scholl. We had expected to meet for just a few hours, but the hours turned into several days. Inge was now sixty-two years old. Calling back the past was painful for her. Even though she herself did not belong to the White Rose, the years of the Third Reich have lost none of their terror for her. She had sensed, more intensely than her brothers and sisters, the dangers threatening the entire family. It must be remembered that in Germany from 1933 through 1945 many people were, to all intents and purposes, powerless hostages, subject to the brute force wielded by Hitler and his henchmen. These henchmen would arrive at daybreak in their long black leather coats, the uniform of the Gestapo, the Secret State Police. The Scholl family's home in Ulm, too, was visited by them. On three occasions Inge was among those taken into custody.

Several times we had to suspend our conversation in the Rotismühle, to begin again the next day. Inge had to overcome the shadows of her own past to help make this book possible. She took part in every phase of its creation. They say that action helps overcome fear; again and again I found that to be true for her.

Together with her sister Elisabeth, Inge helped me get in touch with friends of her dead sister. They told me episodes of Sophie's life I had not known of. Even Fritz Hartnagel, Sophie's boyfriend, agreed—hesitantly at first— to answer questions about their relationship. We owe him thanks for permission to publish for the first time letters she wrote him. The photos and drawings were contributed by Inge from her private collection. Most of them have never been published before.

What came out of these contacts is not a biography in the traditional sense, but rather a description of the stages of Sophie Scholl's life in a sort of collage of reports, letters, documents, testimonies, and photos.

Hermann Vinke   *Hamburg, April 1980*

Life in Nature,
in Spacious Homes,
in the Classroom

"I press my face to the tree's dusky, warm bark . . ."

"No One to Watch Us but the Trees"

The Rotismühle living room has light-colored wainscoting. On the table is a small photo album with glossy black and white pictures of Sophie and her brothers and sisters—so different from the few photos that have been published up to now: a cheerful face, beautifully carved, almost boyish. We—Inge Aicher-Scholl and I—speak of Sophie's childhood in Forchtenberg on the Kocher River in Baden-Württemberg, Germany. Sophie Scholl was born there on May 9, 1921, and lived there for seven years with her brothers and sisters: Inge, born in 1917; Hans, 1918; Elisabeth, 1920; and Werner, 1922. For a moment Inge Aicher-Scholl gives in to bitter melancholy and says softly, "Who can ever foresee what will become of children?" Then she tells me about their childhood years in the small town in the Kocher valley. An almost sane world arises from her memory. Looked at from the standpoint of today's ravaged world, the Forchtenberg of the 1920s, the Scholl's sheltered home, must indeed have been a true paradise for the children.

The surroundings of Forchtenberg were indescribably beautiful. Vineyards and dense mixed forests of beeches and firs encircled the town. We would spend hours, sometimes days, in these forests, picking berries, gathering mushrooms, playing hare and hounds. I clearly remember one particular place, where a humpbacked parsonage garden was right next to the weather-beaten ruin of a castle. With its many different kinds of trees, it resembled a formal park, an ideal place to stage plays. Again and again we thought of new plays to try out, theatrical productions without audiences. There was no one to watch us but the trees.

Stone walls ran all the way up the hillside vineyards in strips. The vintners had probably gathered those rocks over the centuries and used them to subdivide the acreage. On the rock walls there was a riotous growth of all the plants and shrubs that were not allowed to grow among the vines: elders and sloes, little beech trees and firs. We used the stone slabs to fashion entire apartments. Depending on their size and shape, they became tables and chairs, even a piano. Everything was made into something. Small pebbles were cherries, larger ones bowls to put them in. And when a year later we visited our playground, everything was overgrown with moss. Miraculously we became owners of houses filled with moss tablecloths and moss carpets—dense green moss you could grab by the handful.

In our group—my brothers and sisters and girl friends—I was the oldest. Sophie was one of the youngest. She was especially close to our youngest brother, Werner.

They were almost like twins. I can still see them, hand in hand, tripping along barefoot. When we older ones, Hans, Elisabeth and I, started school, Sophie and Werner were more or less left behind.

Today you can hardly go swimming in the Kocher. But in the 1920s it was a perfectly clean river. Near Forchtenberg there was a weir that had a great attraction for us. We would lie on it, basking in the sun, listening to the water splashing by. That was where I taught Sophie to swim. She didn't need much practice. One day, when she was not yet six years old, we swam across the river together for the first time. It was a tremendous experience for Sophie, and somewhat unusual in those days, for schools did not provide swimming lessons.

Sophie came to relish swimming. In fact she felt strongly drawn to water. Whenever she was near a brook or pool, she would take off her shoes and socks and wade barefoot. She just couldn't resist it. And there were plenty of opportunities to wade through water. The Forchtenberg storm drains were in bad repair, and in the spring were often flooded. What gave the grown-ups real headaches meant incomparable pleasure for us children. My father bought stilts for us, and we would cross the flooded streets on them, proud as little kings who had conquered another piece of land.

10

The Parents: Progress and Social Commitment in a Conservative Environment

Sophie's father, Robert Scholl, became mayor of Forchtenberg after having been mayor of the nearby small town of Ingersheim an der Jagst. He made an impressive figure: tall, smoking cigars, and wearing a mustache. His natural authority impressed the children. Even when there were occasional tears, which happens in all families, he was anything but a tyrant. The children were allowed to find their own way. Together with his wife, the former deaconess Magdalene Müller, he created a sheltered island for them in a time of unemployment, inflation, and political violence.

He had grown up in the Mainhardter Woods, a poverty-stricken region farther north. A Protestant pastor had helped the gifted boy to go to high school. During the First World War he was one of the few German pacifists, refusing to share the general war fever, and serving in an ambulance corps. Many years later, as mayor of Forchtenberg, he tried to realize some of his liberal and progressive ideas. Inge Aicher-Scholl, on her parents:

The only link between Forchtenberg and the outside world was an old yellow mail coach which took the townspeople to the railway station on a long, rambling ride. My father refused to put up with this isolation from the world. Against all opposition, he managed to get the Kocher valley railroad extended as far as Forchtenberg. That was his great civic achievement. But beside that, he did a great deal for the towns and for the peasants and artisans of the countryside. He had a gym and a big warehouse built, the latter an agricultural building for storing the harvest; he improved the drainage system, and repaired the streets, badly damaged by flooding.

Many people appreciated his achievements and respected him for it. But among the peasants and artisans there were some who felt differently: "We never had a drainage system before. Why do we need one now, all of a sudden?" they said. Liberal concepts, thoughts of progress and change, were bad things for the conservative peasant, a thorn in the oldtimers' sides. Even the pastor, when he saw him read *Humanity,* a magazine published by the social humanist Friedrich Wilhelm Foerster, one day snarled, "You read that stuff?!" At times my father felt like a stranger in his own town. There was one thing he could not bring himself to do, something which a mayor in that part of the country really had to be able to do: sit in the tavern with the townspeople and wet his whistle. After all, the Kocher valley is a vintners' valley. He never could bring himself to do it, either then nor later. Even as a child I had a distinct feeling—and perhaps Sophie did too—that certain groups were against my father, that they failed to understand his openness to new ideas. We were distinctly aware of their medievalism, in the negative sense.

My parents met during the First World War in a military hospital in Ludwigsburg. Because my father refused to carry a gun, he had been assigned to the Red Cross to care for wounded soldiers. My mother worked as a nurse in the same hospital. She was a cheerful woman, open to people and to life. Later, as the mayor's wife, she fulfilled her social obligations, not because that was what a mayor's wife was supposed to do, but because she genuinely felt compassion for the sick and the poor.

As for us, her children, she was deeply interested in everything we experienced. She lived with us totally. Here is an example of the principles she tried to teach us. I had had a big fight with a classmate, and I asked my mother to come to school with me and give the girl a piece of her mind. She seemed to agree, went to the school yard with me, and then, without a word, she walked away. So there I was, all alone. Eventually I grasped her intended lesson: "Never have someone else intervene in your quarrels. *You* cope with them!"

"My Father Always Rented Big Apartments"

Sometimes Otl Aicher joins us in our talks. He has known the Scholl family since his childhood. He feels Robert Scholl was a great influence on the children, "because he was a liberal man—not free-enterprise liberal the way big businessmen or the German Nationalists were, but devoted to progress and change." The turbulence of the Weimar period was reflected in the polarity between the mayor and the Forchtenberg people. "Political views were displayed openly at that time. You spoke your mind and were not exactly cautious about it. Quite the contrary. Robert Scholl's liberal views were soon the talk of the town."

Otl and Inge disagree as to which parent Hans and Sophie took after. Inge feels that there was a close kinship between Hans and their mother, that Hans was very close to her in his makeup. Otl contradicts her:

I see it quite differently. Physically and mentally Sophie resembled her mother. Look at the physical similarity: the dark eyes, the size—Sophie was shorter than Hans; her body—Sophie was the sportive type, her face almost boyish; her manner—she was the quiet one and, like her mother, really didn't talk much. Hans was more impulsive and more energetic. In that he was more like his father. Their sizes, too, were similar; both Hans and his father were tall.

Robert Scholl was mayor of Forchtenberg until 1930 when the townspeople voted him out. They felt they were being too stirred up from their medieval tranquility. The family of seven moved into a new home in Ludwigsburg and two years later, in 1932, they moved again, to Ulm on the Danube—a big, worldly city compared with Forchtenberg. There Sophie's father started his own business as a tax and financial consultant.

Inge did not feel bothered by those frequent moves.

In Forchtenberg we had a spacious apartment in the town hall. In Ludwigsburg my father rented an apartment large enough for a big family, near the railway station, in a house built around the turn of the century. We had high ceilings and a long hall that led to our bedrooms.

My father always rented big apartments, no matter how badly off we were. He felt everyone should be able to move around freely and be able to get out of everyone's way once in a while. Occasionally my mother would make up for this financial largesse by renting out a furnished room. As an added advantage, the Ludwigsburg apartment was very close to a hunting lodge with an exclusive park. Residents could rent a key and for a few hours enjoy the rare feeling of having a little château and an elegant park all to themselves.

If we wanted to bring home girl friends or the neighbors' children or invite them to a birthday party, there never was a problem. My mother never said, "Today I don't want anyone here—I just scrubbed the floors." They just came along with us. Most of the time there were refreshments, too. Once in a while the girls would sleep over.

In Ulm we had a beautiful, large apartment on the cathedral plaza. In due time it became a popular meeting place for all sorts of friends and acquaintances. From our high windows we could look out on the enormous Ulm cathedral and its plaza, so we always knew what was going on there. And something was always going on there, even if it was just a flight of pigeons tackling the horse droppings.

In a big house like that there was no end of things to do. Books played a most important part in our lives from our earliest childhood. Sophie's first books were Sibylle von Olfers' *When the Root Children Wake Up, Slovenly Peter,* Schnorr von Carolfeld's illustrated Bible, of course Grimms' and Wilhelm Hauff's fairy tales, and most important, the Ludwig Richter book, a fat omnium-gatherum of poems, sayings, fairy tales, and stories, with Richter's [romantic yet cozy] woodcuts. How we cherished that book, even though—or rather, precisely because—many of the poems seemed so enigmatic and fascinating.

16

Sometimes we had open-air classes, with a teacher reading aloud from *Robinson Crusoe*, *Rulaman*, with its cavemen and cave bears, and stories set in the [Bavarian and Swabian] homeland. Later there were poems and prose works by Rainer Maria Rilke, Friedrich Hölderlin, and many other poets.

Sophie liked to play with dolls. My mother, being a great believer in this children's hobby, was particularly good at getting along with dolls. Every Christmas Eve the dolls' house was redecorated, and new dolls' clothes were sewn. When Sophie was older, her Christmas wish was to own a big doll's bed with real wheels so that later, when she had her own baby, it would sleep there.

17

Being Caned,
Or, How She Grew Up

Even during the Weimar Republic, with its first democratic constitution, schools were mainly institutions for teaching submissiveness. Teachers had the right to use corporal punishment for keeping discipline. The teachers frequently acted out their physical superiority by beating the students. Sophie was caned once. Having learned at home to speak up when she disagreed, she couldn't come to terms with inequities occurring at school. She had no trouble with learning in itself, so she was spared many conflicts.

She attended grammar school in Forchtenberg and Ludwigsburg and the girls' high school in Ulm, graduating in March 1940 and thus qualifying for university. Inge relates some events from her sister's school days—samples of how she grew up:

In Forchtenberg a form of caning still existed: The teacher rapped the student's palm with a cane. It was terribly painful and often resulted in a swollen hand. As far as I know, it happened to Sophie only once. Otherwise she had no trouble in school, being a very good student, especially in grammar school. Nor did she have any dif-

ficulty in getting into the girls' high school, which was important for her, since both her sisters, Elisabeth and I, had already achieved this promotion.

In those days a student's status in school was measured not only by grades but also by seating in the classroom. If you excelled in your work, you were moved to a front desk; if you slacked off, you were moved to the back row. At the end of the term, your report card would indicate your seating rank in the class. With all this moving about, my sister Elisabeth—on her birthday, of all days—was demoted by one seat, probably for some rather trivial reason. Sophie was in the same room, since often two or three classes were taught by the same teacher. She became so angry and indignant at the unfairness done to her sister that she went up to the teacher and protested, "Today is my sister Elisabeth's birthday. I'm promoting her back!" The teacher made no objections.

In fact, Sophie felt very strongly about justice. Nor did she lack courage. She would fight back and voice spontaneous protest when she felt someone was being treated unfairly. On the other hand, she tended to be introspective, thoughtful, at times almost shy. Here, for instance, is an episode that occurred in school in Ulm when she was fourteen years old.

She was on a class trip to the valley of the Blau River, a small tributary to the Danube that is framed in some places by steep lime rocks. Not only water, but rocks and trees had always attracted Sophie with an almost

magical power. The teacher was busy explaining something when Sophie climbed the steep rock with almost a sleepwalker's assurance. Once at the top, she looked down happily at her schoolmates, only to see them all staring up at her, horror-stricken. Someone else might have called down,"Come on up!" But she, characteristically responding to their terror, turned around, and very quietly climbed down. She had to promise the teacher never to climb such a dangerous rock again.

She retained this ability of quietly retiring into herself. Unable to blurt out and blast off at any given moment, she took her time to think things over. So when she did say or write something, you felt that reflection.

She Was Proud as a Queen

Growing up, passing from childhood to adolescence, is one of the most difficult phases of life for most people. Many girls consider their first menstruation an important turning point. Inge Aicher-Scholl is quite comfortable discussing this—puberty and sexuality were not taboos in her parental home. Yet she remembers the dejection that she— somewhat more than her sister Sophie—felt during that time:

It may sound odd nowadays, but singing together, making music together—Sophie was quite good at the piano—helped us overcome much of the distress of those years. You could sing away the worries of puberty—the worry of not really knowing where you belong. You are losing your childhood—a rather violent parting—and yet you are not grown up. I used to think: When I turn twenty-one, I'll have made it. But now I must climb and climb and climb to reach the high plain; then no more climbing, peace, the end. What an absurd notion.

I distinctly remember my first menstrual period. We were still in Ludwigsburg. I was transferred to a new class, and they all rushed at me: "Do you have it yet?"

I got rather embarrassed, for I didn't have "it" yet. Then one winter day, sledding in the Ludwigsburg château park, suddenly I felt it: Now I have "it." It really seemed an unpleasant mess. Oddly enough, I was embarrassed to discuss it with my mother, although to her it was a natural and an important thing.

Sophie's turning point was quite different. By that time we had moved to Ulm, and she was about fourteen years old. When her menstrual period came, she was proud as a queen. How interesting and characteristic. Sophie, who was so deeply involved in the life of the mind and the heart, had such strong feelings about her physicality. She relished sleeping, lying in the grass, swimming, and now the distinction of being a woman, symbolized by menstruation. Later on, though, she suffered from painful menstrual cramps. Sometimes she felt depressed about having that pain every time. Also, she felt it was unfair that girls had to bleed and boys did not. Nevertheless, she took these difficulties in her stride, as she generally adapted well to changes. We owed this flexibility to our mother.

Sophie was sick more often than the others, and my mother showed great understanding. Where other mothers might have said, "Come on, off to school with you!" she preferred keeping her child at home. She felt that children should have a chance to sleep as late as they liked once in a while. In the morning she would write a note to the teacher saying that her daughter had been sick. It wasn't a lie, either. At the very least, the child had to have a head cold.

One day I found Sophie in bed—we three sisters shared a large bedroom—and I thought she didn't feel well. But she was sitting up and writing. I asked her, "What on earth are you doing?" and she replied, "I am writing my will." It sounded extremely funny, given the number of belongings we had to bequeath. Thinking back now her list of personal effects was indeed a kind of will. She later put it in the drawer of her night table. The paper no longer exists.

A Declaration of Love for Nature

In her short life, Sophie wrote a great deal. She kept a diary and exchanged numerous letters with acquaintances, friends, and relatives. She wrote compositions and short stories for school and for her own pleasure. Writing was for her a way of clarifying herself and her frame of mind. Writing meant carving thoughts out of a soul. Later, when her friends were at the front, writing letters meant sustaining them, because they were doubly in need of communication.

One of her later compositions, describing a meadow, is an eighteen-year-old's ecstatic, yet by no means exaggerated, declaration of her love for nature:

I can never look at a limpid stream without at least dangling my feet in it; in the same way, I cannot walk past a meadow in May. There is nothing more enticing than a fragrant piece of land. The blossoms of wild chervil float above it like luminous sea spray. Fruit trees lift their branches, blossom-spangled, as if to take flight from this ocean of bliss. No, I just have to abandon my errand, give myself over to the meadow and submerge myself in this rich abundance of diverse life.

27

Oblivious to everything else, I stumble down the slope, luxuriant in its flowers, and am knee-deep amid luscious grasses and flowers. As I kneel down, they brush against my arms. A cool ranunculus touches my cheek. The point of a blade of grass tickles my ear, and for a moment I am covered with gooseflesh, a feeling similar to when a kitten sniffs about my ear with its moist, cold nose. There's a bit of shivering and a bit of sweetness.

Only now can I see all those little beasties living down below the leaves. A tiny beetle enthusiastically puts leg before leg (dear God, six little legs, and not once does he confuse them!) in order to climb up my finger all the way to the tip. And when I turn my hand, he enthusiastically climbs back the same way. So I stop teasing him and put my forefinger close enough to a buttercup for him to step across and be on his way. It's true I cannot actually see it, but I imagine his breast rising in a sigh of relief.

And he is not the only one. All kinds of meadow denizens volunteer to scrabble all over me, on my forehead and nose, up my legs, down my neck. Today I gladly suffer all this, in fact I feel sort of honored that they treat me with such distinction. I lie in the grass, quite still, my arms spread, my knees raised, and am happy. Through the blossoming branches of an apple tree I see the blue sky. Friendly white cloud images float by gently.

All around I feel things budding. I take delight in the wild chervil plants, where little clouds of tiny black beetles dwell, in the red-tinted sorrels, in the slim grasses leaning softly to the east. When I turn my head, it touches the rough trunk of a nearby apple tree. How protectively it spreads its friendly branches over me! Don't I actually feel the continuous flow of the sap from its roots to its tiniest leaf? Could it be I hear a secret throbbing? I press my face to the tree's dusky, warm bark and think, "My homeland," and I am so inexpressibly grateful.

A Green that Could Strike One Dead

It wasn't only through writing that Sophie Scholl expressed her thoughts and feelings. She was also gifted in music and in drawing. Many of her sketches and works have been saved. She did not lack for stimulation. The Scholl family's friends in Ulm included painters and sculptors who were happy to share their talents and ideas, among them Otl Aicher, Bertl Kley, and Wilhelm Geyer. Inge Aicher-Scholl:

Painting and drawing were among our main childhood occupations. Of the five of us, Sophie had the greatest talent. I had flattered myself that I too could accomplish something as a painter; but when I was fifteen, my artistic career came to an end. From then on I acted as Sophie's Maecenas. I bought books, paints, and other painting supplies for her, and sometimes I excused her from dishwashing and drying to give her time to paint. In a certain way she was my protégée. She was the little genius I had to promote.

Ideas and suggestions came from artists who belonged to the family's circle of friends. One of them, Bertl Kley, often invited us to his house. For hours on end he let us gaze at his paintings and discuss colors and plane surfaces with us. On one such occasion he told us how a certain green had almost struck him dead. I can still hear that sentence. Good Lord, I thought at the time, can a color strike one dead? And then I saw that blazing green and was convinced that that green could truly do it.

Best of all, Sophie liked drawing children, probably because she loved children. At first she used very delicate lines. Later she tried watercolors and wax colors. Eventually she started using modeling clay after watching Otl Aicher work. Illustrating long texts was another thing she loved. We would jointly compose a fairy tale, for example. I would write the text and she would supply

the drawings. For one friend she illustrated *Peter Pan*, for another a story by George Heym, "The Afternoon."

Over the years her style changed. At first she did not think very highly of modern art, but under the guidance of another friend of the family, the Ulm painter Wilhelm Geyer, she revised her attitude about expressionism. Much later, when Sophie and Hans attended Munich University, Wilhelm Geyer would secretly work in Munich. The Nazis had ostracized him as a "degenerate artist," a "cultural bolshevist." His central themes were taken from the Old and New Testaments. Some courageous pastors discreetly commissioned his stained-glass windows for their churches. They are among the loveliest things that have survived those years.

My devoting so much of my time to helping Sophie's

artistic career was not meant to patronize her. Nor was I just being solicitous of her needs. It was just such a natural and obvious thing to do. All my brothers and sisters were convinced that artists are something special, and that attention must be paid to their special vocation.

Not that Sophie ever saw herself that way. She didn't view herself as anything special—quite the contrary. She was endowed with an austere unpretentiousness and with a remarkable irony that must have served as a kind of self-protection. This irony saved her from giving herself airs and kept her away from extravagances.

After she graduated from high school, the question arose as to what course of studies Sophie should take. We expected that she would enter an academy of arts, and were flabbergasted when she announced, "Why, art is not something you can *learn*. I'll take biology."

Life Under
the Swastika

"Oh how I wish that just for a little while I could live on an island where I could do and say whatever I wanted to."

"Now Hitler Has Taken Power"

Painting and music took only a small portion of the Scholl children's spare time. Much more of their time was soon taken over by a political youth organization that they at first did not perceive as political at all: the Hitler Youth (*Hitlerjugend*, or HJ). On January 30, 1933, Adolf Hitler had been made chancellor. Robert Scholl, politically aware, had seen the menace of that event, while few other adults felt alarmed. In the preceding years there had been many changes of government. One distinction of the new one was that it made more of an effort to win over the young. The Hitler Youth had existed since 1926, but only in the Third Reich was it made into a broad-based organization. In her book *The White Rose*, published in Germany in 1953, Inge Scholl describes how she experienced January 30, 1933, the day Hitler seized power:

One morning, on the school stairs, I heard one classmate say to another, "Now Hitler has taken power." The radio and all the newspapers proclaimed, "Now everything will be better in Germany. Hitler has seized the helm."

For the first time politics came into our lives. Hans was

fifteen years old at the time, Sophie twelve. We heard a lot of talk about the fatherland, about comradeship, folk community, love of the homeland. That impressed us greatly, and we listened avidly when we heard such talk in school and on the street. For we loved our homeland dearly. . . .

Our fatherland—what was that but the great homeland of all those who shared one language and belonged to one nation? We loved it and could hardly say why. Until now people just hadn't held forth about it. But now it was written across the sky in great, luminous letters. And Hitler, everybody said, would help this fatherland achieve greatness, happiness, prosperity. He would see to it that everybody had work and bread. He would not rest until every last German was independent, free, and happy in his fatherland. We thought that was great, and we were willing to do all we could to help achieve it. . . . We entered [into the Hitler Youth] with body and soul, and we couldn't understand why our father did not approve happily and proudly.

There were vehement family arguments; Inge still remembers them:

Whether we liked it or not, the debates threw a sobering light onto our images of the new age. We talked about the 1920s and how inflation, unemployment, and economic misery had resulted from the First World War.

Our father said, "Once people lose their bare subsistence, once the future looks like nothing but a gray wall to them, they will listen all the more readily to promises without wondering who makes them." Over the next few months we were still sure we could trump his points by reminding him that, clearly, Hitler had kept his promise of doing away with unemployment. And look at that Autobahn achievement! But he said, "Did you stop to think how he is achieving these miracles? He is escalating the war industry. He is building barracks. Can't you see where it will all end? And besides, material security will never satisfy us. After all, we are people who have our own free opinions, our own political ideas, our own beliefs. A government that so much as touches these things is not entitled to our confidence."

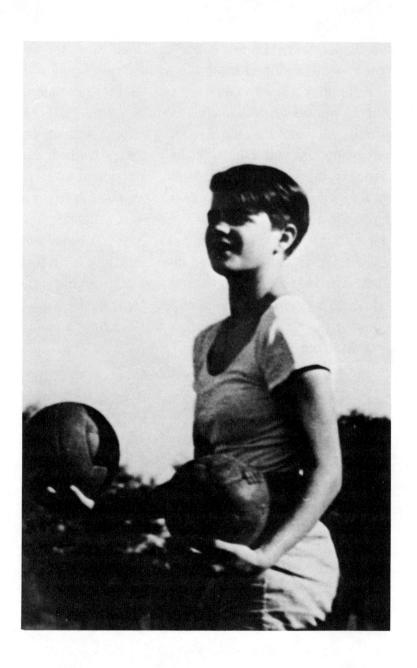

Conflict with the Hitler Youth

At first their father's warnings seemed futile. One after the other, the Scholl children joined the various divisions of the Hitler Youth: first Hans, then Inge, Elisabeth, and finally Sophie and Werner. The divisions were determined by age and sex: The *Jungvolk* for ten-to-fourteen-year-old boys, the *Jungmädel* for ten-to-fourteen-year-old girls. Fourteen-to-eighteen-year-old boys were admitted into the *Hitlerjugend* proper (HJ), girls into the *Bund Deutscher Mädel* (BDM). The three sisters as well as Hans saw their membership as a challenge. The group took them seriously, assigned them tasks, and demanded achievements. Under the motto "Youth led by youth," if you passed muster you could command others. The Scholl children soon became "youth leaders."

The girls' group life was less regimented than the boys'— the Führer deemed training girls less important than training boys—but there were no basic differences. Everything was kept in perpetual motion: uniforms, raising the flag, roll calls, marches, the works. Sophie soon felt troubled when she realized that to a considerable degree these activities were artificial and therefore absurd. And too, the way her Jewish friends and acquaintances were treated caused her great anxiety. Inge tells how the conflict with the HJ started:

As far as I recall it, Sophie was less carried away than Hans and I by the excitement of 1933–34. True, she cheerfully took part in the hustle and bustle of her *Jungmädel* group, in their hiking, camping, and scouting. The solemn speeches by the bonfire, the torchlight songs must have impressed her. But they never took complete possession of her. The need to keep her distance may have been intensified by the perpetual-motion exercises that were supposed to keep everyone breathlessly busy.

I remember that once on a bicycle trip a fifteen-year-old girl suddenly said, "How lovely all this would be if only there wasn't this business about the Jews." There were two Jewish girls in Sophie's class in Ulm, Luise Nathan and Anneliese Wallersteiner, daughters of well-respected families. They were not allowed to join the BDM, which kept enraging Sophie. Again and again she asked, "Why can't Luise, with her fair hair and blue eyes, be a member, while I with my dark hair and dark eyes am a member?" She just could not understand, much less accept, anti-Jewish racism. She deliberately maintained her friendship with Anneliese and often brought her home. She was deeply disturbed by the thought that such a friendship was really forbidden.

There was another episode that bemused her. One day the BDM had its National Youth Day with flags, uniforms, parades. Our group went on a trip to the Swabian mountains. Sophie and I happened on a tent with some boys who were not wearing HJ uniforms. This made us curious. We accosted them and tried to provoke them with our views on National Socialism. But then we noticed that one of the boys pressed his lips together and stopped talking, and all of a sudden we guessed that he was Jewish and had to keep quiet lest he endanger himself and the others. That struck us dumb too, and we took our leave in silence. We felt attracted to people we had been commanded to spurn, and the harder we tried to spurn them, the more intensely they attracted us.

Sophie would listen closely to the frequent arguments between our father and Hans. Hans had a history teacher who must have been a real nationalist. Whenever Hans came home from school and reported how enthusiastically the teacher had spoken of the "Führer," of Germany and the Germans, and how glowingly he contrasted the Germans with the hateful, decadent French, a vehement argument would follow. Again and again my father warned us not to accept everything a teacher said uncritically. But that was exactly what Hans didn't want to hear.

My father was deeply upset by the things he had to watch from his window every day: the eternal parades, the puffed-up carryings-on of the local Nazis, the vicious newspaper articles. He tried to convince his son by appealing to his sense of reality. But Hans could not be

budged. Like every adolescent, he had to go through his own experiences.

The arguments between the two subsided in 1936 after Hans had attended the Nuremberg Party Convention of the National Socialist German Workers' Party (NSDAP)—the Nazi Party. That year he had been chosen to carry the flag of his *Stamm* [his 600-member group]. This was a great honor, and the other members congratulated him. I remember girls telling me, "Your Hans is so handsome. He is just the right boy to carry the flag of his *Stamm*."

When he came home from Nuremberg, my brother was completely changed: tired, depressed, taciturn. He didn't say anything, but we all could tell that something must have happened between him and the HJ. By and by we found out. The inane drill, the paramilitary parades, the silly chatter, the vulgar jokes—all that had exhausted him. From dawn to dusk: Fall in for roll call, listen to speeches, be sure to display enthusiasm. No one had time for a sensible conversation.

What had happened in Nuremberg irritated Sophie and all of us. But Nuremberg did not mean a decisive break yet. It did mean the first crack that was to sever us from the world of Hitler Youth and BDM.

Cross-Country Hitchhiking

In the early 1930s a different youth organization, founded on November 1, 1929, was evolving in the larger German cities: the *"Deutsche Jungenschaft vom 1. November"* (German Boys' League of the First of November). Its members called it simply "d.j.1.11." It was a late offspring of the youth leagues that had arisen around the turn of the century and, in their incarnation as the *Wandervogel* (bird of passage) movement, had rediscovered nature and the environment. Hans became more and more involved in it, though he was still a Hitler Youth member. Inge Aicher-Scholl and her husband, Otl Aicher, describe it to me; Otl Aicher—first:

The d.j.1.11. was illuminated by the openness of the 1920s. It was not nationalistic, nor was it exclusively concerned with nature. Essentially it was open to a new culture and a civilized world. In their very dress and public behavior these young people displayed their urbanity. Not for them the Wandervogel's grubby hiking outfit and backpack, nor the omnipresent bicycle. The boys of the d.j.1.11. preferred to wait at the roadside and hitchhike cross country—not into the Black Forest or the Bavarian mountains but to Sweden, Finland, or Sicily. Theirs was not a homespun life-style but a cultural cosmopolitanism, open to any challenge.

Books played an important part. The boys discovered literature and got involved in what was later called degenerate art. They saw coming to terms with basic philosophical issues as their assignment. Friedrich Nietzsche and Stefan George were important subjects. In fact every new book meant new discovery. They would read to each other late into the night, discuss what they had heard, and plan the next reading.

If the Wandervogel movement had attempted to introduce youth, and along with it, society, to alternative life views and new choices, the d.j.1.11. took an additional step. Inge Aicher-Scholl describes it this way:

The d.j.1.11. had a fascinating style, comparable to the "Bauhaus," the new directions of architecture and art in the 1920s. To give a few examples: The members spurned capital letters [like the poets Stefan George and e.e. cummings]; they loved lyrical poetry and wrote poems themselves; they staged plays; they sang unforgettable choral songs, setting mostly Russian or Scandinavian poetry to music. On weekends, even in winter, they would set out carrying Lapp-style tents. They lit fires, brewed tea, and lived a life of their own. Independent of church denomination, party, parents, and school, the group also called itself the Autonomous Boys' League. Hans belonged to it, and later Ernst Reden, a young writer from Cologne who had to do his military service in Ulm.

Soon after Hitler assumed power in January 1933, the free youth movement, including the d.j.1.11., was banned. The Nazis could not tolerate any independent youth organizations competing with HJ and BDM. But it was right in the face of this ban, in Ulm and other German cities, that d.j.1.11. groups developed around boys like Hans Scholl who could no longer think along the cramped, nationalistic lines of the HJ. As Otl Aicher puts it, "The HJ had eyes and thoughts only for things German, only for the German nation and its mission of subjugating the world." The boys, growing ever more disenchanted, ever more critical, needed the cohesion of their own group. Far from the official Nazi activities, they organized regular meetings. They read banned poetry, exchanged prints and picture postcards by proscribed painters—coveted collector's items—and sang the songs tabooed in the HJ: Russian, Scandinavian, Gypsy songs. The songs were mimeographed and collected in gray-and-red binders. Each boy owned one of these binders.

Inge and Sophie Scholl did not belong to the d.j.1.11. because it was only for boys twelve years old and over. But they came to know this shared style of life and were influenced by it. Inge Scholl again:

With the establishment of this group, for Hans and Werner Scholl and for their sisters too, a new social framework replaced the family as a major influence, even though it happened inside the family home. The boys had their retreat. Our mother was allowed to serve them pastry and gallons of tea; no other intrusion was tolerated. The boys' world was so alien to our father that he kept out of the way when they were conversing in their own language.

We three sisters could take part only indirectly in this boys' league. But through them we were introduced to new books; we sang their songs; and we knew a lot about their hikes, even though we could not go along with them.

Riding to Stuttgart by Open Truck

The Secret State Police, the Gestapo, had long been track-
ing down the d.j.1.11.'s illegal activities. Late in the fall
of 1937 it got ready to put its foot down. All over Germany
young people were arrested, including the children of Robert
Scholl, tax and finance consultant in Ulm. Prosecution for
plotting subversive activities in outlawed associations was
started. Inge Scholl, along with her sister Sophie and her
brothers Hans and Werner, got to know jail for the first
time. She reports:

One early morning in November 1937, the doorbell
rang. "Gestapo! Open the door!" The two men had orders to search the apartment and take the children into
custody. My parents were shocked. They could not imagine that there were serious charges against us. But my
mother kept her presence of mind. If indeed something
was the matter, it could concern only the two boys. She
took a basket and told the officers, "Excuse me, gentlemen, I am in a hurry to get something from the bakery."
That sounded all right to the "gentlemen." Why should
the woman's presence be needed?

She left the room and went up to the top floor where

the boys' room was. There she put whatever might look suspicious into the basket and took it to neighbors. When she came back, the officers had finished their search and were about to take the children. My mother let fly at them. Dear Lord, what a sudden burst of eloquence! But her fury was of no avail. Sophie, Werner, and I were taken away. Hans was doing his military service at the time and had been arrested in the barracks. They kept us in jail for a day, in separate cells of course. Sophie had been released immediately. The officers had taken her inadvertently, thinking that she was a boy.

On the evening of that memorable day Werner and I, along with the other boys who had been arrested, were taken by open truck from Ulm to Stuttgart on the newly built Autobahn. It was quite a terrible [fifty-mile] ride, with no warm clothes, in a snowstorm across windswept mountains. In Stuttgart each of us was put in a cell, and no one knew what was going to happen.

Sitting in my cell, I couldn't help thinking of June 30, 1934, of Hitler's bloody vendetta against SA leaders, of Ernst Röhm and other leading Nazis, shot for alleged conspiracy. At the time I had thought: How terrible that all of a sudden he has people put to death who used to be his friends, possibly just because of some misunderstanding. And now, three years later, there I was in jail myself. Above and below I heard steps, creaks, doors slamming. Who knows, I thought, perhaps Father and Mother have been arrested too, and what if there is another misunderstanding like the one in 1934?

We were kept locked up for a week—no reading and no working permitted—then called to be interrogated. Two Gestapo officers took turns. When one ran out of questions, the other took over. One question was, "Have you ever heard of a resistance group?" I said, "Yes, I read about it in the papers." They were thinking about the case of Ernst Niekisch, editor of *Resistance* magazine, who had been arrested a short time before. The officer insisted, "And what did you think about it?" I said, "I think it is a group of friends who have got together to fight evil." They roared with laughter—they couldn't believe such imbecility. And I thought it was just as well that they were laughing, and laughed with them. When they asked, "In your apartment there were those gray-and-red binders. What can you tell us about them?" My answer was: "I think gray and red is a nice color combination." Another roar of laughter, which may have been fortunate for me. The gray-and-red binders were of course those of the d.j.1.11.

Finally, after the interrogation, they released us. My mother had heard about it and had come to Stuttgart to pick us up. When we saw her in the prison anteroom, relaxed, carrying an afternoon snack for us, I couldn't help thinking: This is so typical of our mother.

We visited some friends in Stuttgart and then went home to Ulm with her. My brother Hans was in jail for almost five weeks. Key figures like him and Ernst Reden, who had been arrested at the same time, were kept longer. Hans' commanding officer was an understanding captain who showed up at the jail again and again and told the Gestapo, "Hans Scholl is ours. If there is something to be taken care of, we will take care of it." He got Hans released. However, Ernst Reden, whom we all greatly admired at the time—he was the literary character—was kept in the Welzheim concentration camp for more than six months.

The fact that we had been in jail was of course prejudicial to Sophie. In school they kept bringing it up and asking her, "What on earth have you people been up to?" I don't know exactly what she replied, but at any rate she was very proud. She had an attitude that my brother Hans expressed later on in Russia when my mother wrote and asked him to submit a petition for clemency on behalf of our father, who at that time was in jail. Hans declined, explaining, "We must bear it in a different spirit from other people. This is a distinction!" Sophie too, I believe, felt that our jailing had been a distinction.

Here I have to mention our parents once again. Our family at that time was a sheltering island. Since Hans' arrest, the fights between him and my father had stopped altogether. After dinner we used to go for walks, preferably strolling along the Danube. While Hans was still in jail, we children often went for walks with our father. I could sense how hard he had been hit by our imprisonment. One night, as Sophie and he and I were walking arm in arm, he gave vent to his feelings. Squeezing my arm, he said, "If those bastards harm my children in any way, I'll go to Berlin and shoot him," meaning Hitler. Later, when Hans and Sophie were dead and we, the survivors, were in jail once again, I often thought: How impossible to go to Berlin and shoot the man who had harmed the children! How powerless we were! But he did say it, and I never forgot it. You don't forget such an outcry, because it gives you the feeling that you are standing on granite, that someone is with you, an important feeling in times like those.

Indeed, we children sensed more and more strongly than ever that the ground beneath our feet had become porous and unsafe. After my imprisonment, when I no longer belonged to the BDM, one day another member told me, horrified, what had happened at one leadership conference Sophie had participated in. A high-level leader had come from Berlin specifically to discuss with the girls what they should read at their weekly meetings. As if it were the most obvious thing in the world, Sophie had suggested Heinrich Heine. She was surprised at the harshness with which the others rejected her idea. Wasn't Heine a Jewish poet? Sophie had said, almost inaudibly, "He who doesn't know Heinrich Heine doesn't know German literature."

"She Danced with Great Abandon"

The shock of the arrests had its aftereffects for a long time. In its wake, Hans and Inge Scholl broke with National Socialism for good. Sophie, being younger, wasn't quite ready yet. It took longer for her personal experiences to mature into a decision. Several times she was hauled before the school administration, which—as she would tell the family somewhat amused yet at the same time disturbed—was trying to uncover in her some secret taint, membership in a clandestine league or something similar. This scrutiny rather helped enhance her self-confidence. At the weekly BDM meetings she felt more and more aloof, particularly since membership had been made compulsory. Hitler Youth was State Youth. In her spare time she continued drawing and painting and, like other young girls, went dancing. Inge distinctly recalls the hit songs of those days.

We went together to carnival balls and artists' balls. The tango, fox-trot, and English waltz were fashionable at the time. There were a great many hit songs easy to dance to. Some of them can still be heard once in a while, for instance, "I'm dancing straight into heaven with you." Unlike me, Sophie was an excellent dancer. She danced with great abandon; she let the music carry her away, oblivious to her surroundings, truly going along with her partner. In one of her letters she mentioned that a schoolmate had objected to her "indecent way of dancing." She couldn't help it, she said, if other people considered it indecent. For her, dancing meant liberation.

Many other afternoons we spent at a friend's place. Anneliese had a phonograph and dance records. Sophie and Fritz Hartnagel met there in 1937. Sophie was sixteen years old, Fritz twenty. He had just graduated from the Potsdam military academy and was serving as cadet in Augsburg [some fifty miles from Ulm]. What had attracted him to the army was the notion of chivalry, which he associated with an army officer's career. Moreover, as Fritz explained to me, among the officers there was a discernible aloofness from the Party. He, too, had come from the youth movement. Now that it had been outlawed, he felt that its notion of an elite ruled by moral obligation was embodied in the officers' corps. Over the years Sophie and Fritz's fleeting acquaintance grew into a close friendship. Frequent partings and then the war did not destroy it. Since they could rarely see each other, there were many letters, most of them written by Sophie. This contact became vitally important to her.

I ask Inge whether themes like love, friendship, and sex had been tabooed in the group she and Sophie belonged to. Her reply:

I don't believe that sex was a taboo subject. It didn't need to be, because it had a different value from today's. It didn't have that central importance. As far as I remember, we mostly called it eroticism, and we usually associated it with love. Love had a whole universe of meanings. It implied tenderness in the slightest touch of your little finger, tenderness in your eyes.

Love existed in every object there was, and so it existed in physical tenderness and in what today seems to be the foremost need, in sexual union. We didn't disparage that union, but we didn't give it first importance either. We could enjoy waiting. Waiting and knowing that we were growing together was a pleasure in itself. I know that to young people this must sound hopelessly old-fashioned. But I am deliberately telling it as it was and as I wish it could still be.

To show you how little taboo there was about sexual things: Sophie and I always shared a bedroom, a true girls' room, with a narrow aisle between the beds, with a night stand next to each bed, a washbasin, a few pictures on the wall, and the ever-present doll's cradle. A year before Sophie graduated from high school, they had sex education in biology class. One night she said, "Listen, today we had a terrific lesson. I want to explain it to you." She slid under my blanket, took a pad and a drawing pencil, and in great detail drew what the biology teacher had taught them. In her sober enthusiasm she made up for what I, four years older than she, had not caught on to in school.

In his book *The Meaning of Hitler—Hitler's Use of Power—His Successes and Failures,** Sebastian Haffner makes some observations on sex, friendship, and love in the Third Reich. The chapter "Achievements" lists among other things the revolutionizing of sexual morality and women's emancipation. Haffner says:

"In actual fact, [the women's movement] made great leaps forward, especially during the second six-year span of the regime, during the war, and then with the full approbation and often vigorous support of party and state. Never before had women moved into so many male occupations and male functions as during the Second World War, and this process was no longer reversible—and probably would not have been reversible even if Hitler had survived the Second World War."

Of course those "moves into male functions" were due to the war. It is highly doubtful that those "moves" promoted true equality for women. There had been some progress in women's liberation in the 1920s; it was followed by "great leaps" backward. As we know, Hitler never had much use for women. They were just tools for

---

* Translated by Ewald Osers. New York: Macmillan, 1979. p. 36.

his political purposes. "Girls' training was primarily supposed to make them into mothers who joyfully insisted on having lots of babies," comments Inge Aicher-Scholl. "Hitler would need their offspring as cannon fodder and as the colonial masters of eastern Europe. That was the only reason he put mothers on a pedestal."

Books: First Intimations of Resistance

Sophie Scholl read a great deal and had many friends at that time. Inge Aicher-Scholl explains:

The books we were reading—whether by Thomas Mann, Bernard Shaw, Stefan Zweig, Werner Bergengruen, or Paul Claudel—like modern art, turned into bills of indictment against society. They made us confront Natonal Socialism. They mobilized our defiance.

Those books, however, were not gifts from heaven—they came from the hands of young friends. At that time our circle of friends was crucially important in Sophie's life. Friendship came to mean solidarity in fending off the Hitler state. I remember the wife of Bertl Kley, the painter, saying, "We have a wide circle of friends, and all of them are against Hitler. And each of these friends, in turn, has a circle of friends who are against Hitler, and so on, and so on, a huge subterranean network against Hitler. If we could only get that network into joint action . . . "

The friends told one another about books. I daresay these books became the first intimations of resistance. But more than that, the friends began to reach conclusions. They came to grasp that experience arises not

from what you read, but from what you do. Books could stimulate, could impart an insight, could light a candle. But all of this would be relevant to your own life, your true self, only when you put into practice what you had determined was right.

It therefore was incisive for all of us when Otl Aicher, who had never been a member of the Hitler Youth, refused to join it just because the school board wanted him to right before his final high school exams. Many a well-meaning adult, with a [well-meaning] wink, urged him to accommodate: Just a formality, a few days' membership rather than hazard your graduation! But for him it was not a mere formality. He persisted.

He was one of the friends who had handed us books

like Socrates' *Apology*, Saint Augustine's *Confessions*, Pascal's *Pensées*, Maritain's *Antimoderne,* and others. During the last years of Sophie's life, he was one of her most important comrades. So was her younger brother, Werner.

When Hans was drafted and Elisabeth was getting her vocational training, only Sophie and Werner were left at home, as in the years of their childhood. Werner was devoted to Sophie, and we owe him for the finest photographs of her. In his room, which was a bit out of the way, he started building a small library on religions of the world. As early as his d.j.1.11. days, he had come upon Lao-tze. Now he added Buddha, Confucius, Sanskrit writings, the Koran, then the Greek philosophers. Through his friend Otl Aicher he discovered the testimonies of early Christianity and the great Christian luminaries. Thus, Werner was the first of us to be intensely preoccupied with Christianity.

As a sideline, he was involved in quite different activities, mostly at night. For instance, one morning the monumental stone statue of Justitia in front of the Ulm courthouse was found blindfolded with a swastika flag, which we learned later had been supplied by Werner. Another time, on the occasion of a Nazi celebration, he put firecrackers next to the official speaker's lectern and was successful far beyond any expectation.

The Moon Battling the Clouds
Or, "But I Would So Much Rather Have Cake"

During the last two years before she graduated from high school in March 1940, there were, at least on the surface, no major conflicts for Sophie. She paid just enough attention in class to maintain her grade level. "Sometimes," she wrote in a letter, "school is like a film—a film I watch but can hardly act in." She gave that impression of "total non-participation in class" to her biology teacher, Dr. Else Fries. Her teacher added, though, that whenever she asked Sophie a question she was immediately alert and knew the answer.

Outside school, Sophie pursued her artistic hobbies: drawing, occasionally ceramics. In November 1938 she wrote to a friend that in her life studies class she still had to draw men. The painting teacher had told her that in life studies men were the bread and women the cake. Sophie added: "But I would so much rather have cake!" In summer, swimming was her favorite activity, but she also liked just being outdoors and, standing under a tree, "letting herself go." If anything, her relationship to nature grew more intimate. She would admire the equanimity of roses and discover unsuspected aspects of the wind: "Here on the cathedral plaza the wind indulges in jokes so droll

that it would be stupid not to laugh."

In the summer of 1938 she, some of her friends, and her brother Werner, took a vacation on the North Sea, where among other things they went through a stormy trip on a trawler. The next summer she stayed at the artists' village Worpswede near Bremen for a few days. Several artists let her watch them work. In the Bremen State Museum she became familiar with the paintings of Paula Modersohn-Becker, whom she deeply revered. She was told that Heinrich Vogeler, whose delicate paintings introduced her to *Jugendstil (Art Nouveau)*, had left Germany.

65

She never felt quite comfortable with the people of northern Germany. Traveling there, she soon got homesick for her Swabian southland. She planned her vacations as early as possible and saved her allowance with iron persistence. Sometimes she would think herself into a far remote future: "If possible, I will live in the country. I don't think city life agrees with me."

Her relationship with Fritz Hartnagel gradually grew closer and firmer, although at first she had anticipated something very different. She had wanted Fritz to be one of her friends, nothing more. But her feelings overruled what her reason desired. In her letter of November 7, 1939 (two months after Hitler started the war), she described to Fritz her role in their relationship.

I can think of you quite calmly. And I am glad to be able to do so the way I like it, without any obligation. How exquisite when two people can have a relationship without having to promise: Let's meet at such and such a place, or let's always stay together. They simply walk part of the road together. If it so happens that their roads diverge, each continues calmly in his own direction.

In another letter, written November 28, 1939, she says,

As long as I have neither you nor mail from you, every evening I think of our stroll on that narrow path along the Danube. Since then there has been moonlight almost every

night. Do you remember the moon battling the clouds?
Tonight it is round and blurry, with a huge halo, its outer
rim all the colors of the rainbow.

The moon battling the clouds—a lovely image which
says something about the relationship between Sophie and
Fritz. There were no possessive claims between them.
Both used sparingly the tenderness and the feelings they
had for each other. At one point Sophie wrote she was
scared of awakening and nurturing in her friend something
that might have to die. She sensed how fragile the relationship was, how easily the war and political events could
destroy it. In her letter of November 28 she continued,

Dearest Fritz,

This whole letter may seem very strange to you. You may have so much to see and do that you have no time left to think of yourself. So I am a little scared. You do think of me sometimes in the evening, don't you? Do you sometimes dream of our vacation? But do not think of me only the way I am. Think also of the way I would like to be. Only then, if you love me just as dearly, will we be able to understand each other completely. We don't really know each other well enough, and to a great degree that is my fault. I always was aware of it and was too contented to do something about it. Please don't believe that this will come between us, for I am trying very hard to be with you in my thoughts, to simply hold on to you. But neither do I believe that during a war this is unimportant. Grave adversity is no reason for people to let themselves go. My dearest, do understand me, and pardon me for whatever in this letter seems clumsy. Perhaps many of my words are fatuous, hurtful, superfluous. Remember that my judgment is based on my own feelings, that perhaps I am translating what I am into what you are. From all my heart,

> *Yours,*
>
> *Sophie.*

"Do Not Say It Is for the Fatherland"
Letters Against the War

In retrospect it is not possible to say exactly when Sophie renounced National Socialism for good. During her last two years of high school, seemingly such carefree years, she arrived at a clear-cut attitude toward the Nazi regime. Besides what she saw in her surroundings, historical events were breaking forth one right after the other. She followed them with the greatest attention: Austria being forcefully annexed (*Anschluss*) in March 1938; then early in October the German troops invading the Sudetenland of Czechoslovakia; on November 9 the so-called *Reichskristallnacht*, the Night of Broken Glass, an officially organized assault on Jews and Jewish establishments all over Germany—arousing consternation and anger in the Scholl family; after the *Kristallnacht* the end of the Spanish Civil War, which Robert Scholl had followed closely on the Swiss radio as a frightening omen of terrible things to come; and eventually, with the invasion of Poland, September 1, 1939, the Second World War.

All of Sophie's friends who were drafted had to promise her never to shoot. But she knew full well how unrealistic such a promise was. There are bitter lines in a letter to her friend Fritz Hartnagel. "Now of course there will be enough for you people to do. I cannot comprehend it, human beings constantly putting other human beings into mortal danger, over and over again. I will never understand it; I think it is horrible. Do not say it is for the fatherland."

A few days later she told her friend what she thought the chances for peace were: "We do not indulge in the hope of an early end to the war even though they say here, childishly, that Germany's blockade will force England to surrender. We will have to see. . . ."

Fritz was still stationed in Germany. Sophie's letters to him over the following weeks sounded more and more urgent. She had deeply disapproved of and condemned the things that had happened to her family, to the Jews, to dissenters, in the years before 1939. The war intensified that reaction and aroused her feelings about right and wrong. From now on she would no longer keep quiet and keep her rage to herself, least of all in speaking to the man she loved, an army officer in this war. In her letter of June 22, 1940, she told him the plain truth: If their views on the war were radically opposite, she could not envision a life with him. She wrote:

I am only too happy to believe that when we discuss philosophical issues and, closely related to them, political issues, you contradict me merely because you like to disagree. I know that motivation; one loves disagreeing. But I myself have never contradicted you just for the sake of contradiction, though you may secretly believe that I did. On the contrary, I always leaned over backward in deference to your profession. After all, you are bonded to that profession and possibly, because of it, weigh these things more carefully. Perhaps you make compromises once in a while, this way or that way.

I cannot imagine that people could live together if their views on those issues differed, or at least their activities differed.

Just because things are conflicted, man should not himself be in conflict. And yet, all the time and everywhere we hear it said—since we have been put into this conflicting world, we have to adapt to it. Oddly enough, we often find this completely un-Christian opinion espoused by, of all people, so-called Christians. How then can we expect fate to make a righteous cause prevail when there is hardly anyone who unequivocally gives himself up to a righteous cause?

I recall a story from the Old Testament. All day long and all night long Moses stood holding up his arms praying to God for victory. And whenever he let down his arms, the enemy prevailed over the children of Israel. Are there still people today who never weary of directing all their thinking and all their energy, unequivocally, to one cause? I cannot claim, though, that I am one of those "poor in spirit" in the true sense of the word. There has hardly been an hour where not a single thought of mine wavered from the struggle. Only in a minuscule fraction of my activities

*have I been doing what I regard as the right thing to do. I
often shudder thinking of all those activities looming higher
and higher all around me like the blackest mountains, so
that I am left with only one desire: to not exist, or to exist
as a mere crumb of soil, a little scrap of tree bark. But this
wish, often overwhelming, is another bad thing. It is merely
caused by fatigue.*

*Fatigue is the biggest thing I own. It keeps me silent when
I should speak up, when I ought to confess the concerns I
have about the two of us. I put it off: sometime later. Oh,
how I wish that just for a little while I could live on an
island where I could do and say whatever I liked and didn't
have to be patient for immeasurable ages!*

Sophie Scholl wrote more letters. She argued against
the war, against her friend's interpretation of soldiery.
They tell the soldier, she said, to obey and to take an oath
of allegiance—today to one government, tomorrow to another. How could he be loyal, upright, unassuming, and
sincere when he was given contradictory orders? "According to everything I know about you, you are not exactly for war either, yet all this time you have been training
people for war." In a letter of September 23, 1940, Sophie
used an analogy to spell out what she meant:

To me, a soldier's duty to his country seems something

like a son's to his father and his family. Supposing he has taken an oath that he will stick by his father or his family, no matter what. Now supposing the father wrongs another family and thereby gets into trouble, and the son has to stick with his father, no matter what. I am sorry, I cannot muster that much understanding for kinship. I feel that righteousness must always have a higher value than any, often sentimental, attachment.

It would be ever so much more appealing if people in a dispute could join the side they consider righteous.

I always thought it was wrong for a father to side with his children no matter what. And I think it is just as wrong for a German or a Frenchman to mulishly defend his country merely because it is his country. Emotions can be very misleading. When I see soldiers marching on the street, I feel moved too, especially when there is music. I once used to have to fight off tears. But those are old-wives' emotions; to be ruled by them is ludicrous.

In school they told us that a German's attitude to his country is deliberately subjective and partisan. Unless it is deliberately objective, impartial, and evenhanded, I can't accept it. But this subjective attitude seems plausible to many people, and some who were eager to organize their conflicting emotions adopted it with a sigh of relief.

"We Have to Lose the War"
An Officer Has to Be Consistent:
Either For Hitler or Against Hitler

Former army officer Fritz Hartnagel, today a judge in
Stuttgart, had at first refused to talk about his friendship
with Sophie Scholl, saying that it is his private business.
However, at the request of his son, a history teacher, he
finally agreed to an interview.

I set up the tape recorder in his Stuttgart apartment.
Born in 1917, of medium height, with wavy, dark, gray-
flecked hair, Fritz Hartnagel anticipates my questions with
skeptically alert eyes. His wife, Elisabeth, née Scholl, joins
in on the conversation, which at first moves rather hesitantly. He says that his relationship with Sophie was a
normal friendship. Before the war they used to go on trips
into the mountains, using his father's car—"a beautiful
car, a Wanderer." Once in a while, because of shortage
of gasoline, the trips ended not quite according to plan.
Elisabeth Hartnagel nods yes; she went along on some of
those trips. Fritz Hartnagel says we shouldn't make Sophie
Scholl into a saint. She was a girl like other girls. Then
he talks about the hard decision that he, a professional
soldier, had to make at her request.

As to politics, Sophie was the one that set the trend.
We often debated, and at first did not agree on anything.

75

Only after much hesitation and reluctance did I find myself ready to follow her ideas. What a tremendous plunge for me to take—to say in mid-war, "I am against this war," or "Germany has to lose this war." But it wasn't only Sophie—I too had seen a great many things over the years that made me stop and think: opponents of the Nazi regime put in "protective custody" starting in 1933; later the persecution of Jews, which we directly witnessed in the Scholl house. As a tax consultant, Robert Scholl had frequent contacts with Jews. Some of them had to give up their businesses; others just disappeared.

The widow of one Jewish physician often came to visit. Her husband had been highly decorated in the First World War. Every year he received handwritten birthday congratulations from the mayor of Ulm. In short, the family was part of the city's elite. The woman simply could not understand that under the new rulers she was nothing, that she could no longer build her life on yesterday's assets. One day she brought her family album, with photographs of her late husband, to the Scholls, and gave me a pistol, saying it might be safest with me, an army officer. A few days later she was taken to a concentration camp.

I was particularly shaken by the persecution of Jews that escalated, in the *Reichskristallnacht* of November 9, 1938, into an explosion of violence, with officially organized assaults on Jews, Jewish businesses, and synagogues. In the army I personally did not come across killer commandos, but on a train ride in Russia I overheard officers telling of mass shootings, making it sound like the most natural thing in the world to shoot Jews. I was deeply shocked, as I suddenly became an eyewitness to reality. Up to then, on so-called enemy broadcasts, I had occasionally heard of atrocities and mass shootings, but I had remained skeptical and didn't know whether the reports were propaganda or truth. Gradually I realized that I was serving as a soldier of a criminal's regime. But the decision to change sides, even if only mentally, took time. It could not be made overnight.

Sophie was not a coldly calculating woman and could be very emotional. Still she thought things through with acute intelligence and logical consistency. One example: During the winter of 1941–42 a major propaganda action asked the German population to donate warm clothes and other woolen things to the army. The German soldiers, in their drive on Leningrad and Moscow, were mired in a winter campaign for which they were not prepared. The people were asked to donate coats, blankets, and skis. But Sophie stated her position: "We won't give." At the time I had just come from the Russian front to Weimar to put together a new company. When I heard of Sophie's harsh stand, I tried to draw her a picture of what that attitude would mean to the soldiers out there: they had no gloves, no sweaters, no warm socks. But she was adamant and gave me her reason: "Whether at this moment it's German soldiers who freeze to death or Russians makes no difference; it's all equally bad. We have to lose the war. If we donate woolens now, we help prolong it."

I was shocked. We argued vehemently. Step by step I came to admit that her attitude was correct. You can either be for Hitler or against Hitler. If you were against Hitler, you had to see to it that he lost the war. Only a military defeat could overcome him. And that in turn meant that whatever aided the so-called enemy and hurt us Germans—that alone could bring back our freedom.

The Fröbel Seminary
Or, "Exposing All Those Lies"

In March 1940 Sophie easily passed her final exam. It had been an annoying hurdle, but no more important to her than her passing from one grade to the next. Just before the exam she had played hookey; Fritz Hartnagel had gotten a short leave, and they went on a trip into the mountains.

After graduation Sophie would have loved to start biology and philosophy classes right away. But there was a prerequisite: six months' duty with the National Labor Service (*Reichsarbeitsdienst,RAD*), whose last-but-not-least purpose was to supply cheap labor, since labor was getting scarcer and scarcer. To avoid the Labor Service, Sophie registered at the Fröbel Seminary for kindergarten teachers in Ulm, to start in early May 1940. She used the eight weeks between graduation and training to go on bicycle trips with her sister Inge or her best friend, Lisa Remppis. After one such trip she reported that they had felt like "God's officials," sent out to see if the earth was still good, "and we found it very good."

Training at the Fröbel Seminary required a major readjustment and a lot of hard work. Sophie loved children, but she was not used to dealing with them as a group on

79

a daily basis. She took her new job very, very seriously. For her own purposes, she wrote down evaluations of her pupils and tried to figure out why some of the little ones were slow in learning to talk. These descriptions, too, showed how closely she observed, and how accurately she could put her observations into words and delineate the little ones' faces. Nor did she exclude herself from these descriptions. At one point she noted that she was not yet relaxed enough or patient enough to deal with children.

In August 1940, for her practical training, she had a four-week working vacation in a children's home in Bad Dürrheim in the Black Forest. Run by a seventy-year-old former major and his forty-five-year-old wife, the home cared for children and adolescents with stomach and intestinal diseases. The older ones especially gave Sophie

some trouble at first. After all, she was a kindergarten teacher-to-be. Most of the patients seemed to Sophie arrogant, stupid, spoiled, and narrow-minded. They came from a so-called better social background; working-class families could not afford such an expensive home in such a famous spa.

The living conditions, too, tried Sophie's patience. She had to share her tiny room with a hysterical girl who would laugh out loud in the night, without rhyme or reason—that is, when she didn't happen to be snoring. She had "a brain like a hen's and 145 pounds of unappealing flesh," as Sophie wrote her sister Elisabeth. The girl bathed once every four weeks and, on top of it all, considered herself a beauty.

The spate of letters from Bad Dürrheim continued during her weeks in the children's home. She wrote to her friends at the front, her two sisters, her friend Lisa, her brothers, her parents. She covered everyone, and everyone was admonished not to keep her waiting for an answer. Again and again in her letters one sentence recurs: "I hope you'll write me very soon." Like a soldier in the service, she counted the days of her assignment. At last, in September, she returned to Ulm and to the Fröbel Seminary to continue her training.

National-Socialist politics were not about to abate for kindergarten teachers, however. One of her classmates, Susanne Zeller, née Hirzel, daughter of an Ulm minister, remembered those days in a letter to Inge Scholl dated August 27, 1979.

Most of the time Sophie was reticent, quiet, and rather introspective. She spoke in a low voice. Some people thought she was almost shy. But if you knew her, you could tell that she definitely was self-confident and rightly felt superior to some of the others, though she never let them feel it. She kept her distance. You felt sure her center of gravity was somewhere else, not in this kindergarten job.

One day we *Jungmädel* leaders were called together and solemnly divested of our office. (We sang the song, "Where we stand, stands loyalty.") Why? We had decorated our *Jungmädel* flag with our own symbols. But,

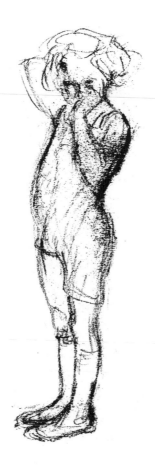

the authorities generously added, they didn't mean to
fatally obstruct our future. They allowed us to stay in a
Nazi outfit as BDM girls. Sophie thought the whole group
was nauseating, imbecilic, and dishonest. "We really ought
to fawn our way up, dissemble our way up to high office,
and then expose all the lies." I am mentioning this be-

cause the question: "What can we do?" arose quite early on.

Viewed from the outside, our year at the Fröbel Seminary was quite uneventful. We saluted the flag, for instance, only when we had to. The seminary head, Miss Kretschmer, was not an all-out National Socialist. She knew how to appear noncommittal. So one day when we were supposed to listen enthusiastically, in a "community reception," to a Hitler speech on the radio, we dared to read our books openly. Miss Kretschmer noticed our lack of interest and merely warned us by waving a finger. She could have reacted quite differently.

We were living on two different levels, you might say. On one level, we were cheerful and carefree. I remember, for instance, our farewell party on graduating from the Fröbel Seminary. We staged a pantomime of Schiller's "Glove" with a speaker reciting the verses. Sophie wholeheartedly shared our exuberance. Her spirit and her talent as a designer helped us compose, in the Scholl apartment on Cathedral plaza, poems and drawings about our classmates, which were then presented like gothic ballads. On the other level, we were highly skeptical and felt insecure. This war, this Nazi party, this stupefaction of people—where would it all end?

Doing Labor Service
Or, "We Live Like Prisoners"

Early in March 1941 Sophie Scholl passed her exam and
graduated as a kindergarten teacher. Now at last, a year
after finishing high school, she could start her university
studies! But that was a vain hope. The authorities refused
to recognize the Fröbel Seminary as a substitute for the
National Labor Service. Four short weeks after the exam
she had to put on the RAD uniform and report to the
Krauchenwies labor camp near Sigmaringe on the upper
Danube. The camp had been established in a somewhat
decrepit castle adjacent to a large formal park. The following six months were often very painful for Sophie. To
begin with, she suffered from homesickness and cold. But
much worse, the drills, harassment by superiors, and the
girls' constant babble set her teeth on edge and strained
her patience and adaptability. "We live like prisoners; for
not only work but time off is made into service," she wrote
in a letter, adding that she could enjoy privacy only when
she took her shower in the evening and when she wrote
and received mail. She bitterly complained that her leader
addressed and treated the girls as "labor maids." "Sometimes I wish I could yell at her, 'My name is Sophie Scholl!
Remember that!' "

85

She deliberately kept her distance from the other girls, making friends with only a very few. She said that men were the only, the most frequent, the most popular subject they discussed, and sometimes that nauseated her. She tried hard to be fair to the girls, even in her thoughts. But she ended up judging them harshly, possibly because of the setup: "Not a very good average."

She was aware that the others thought her stuck up because every precious second of her spare time, and at night in bed with a flashlight, she spent reading books like Thomas Mann's *Magic Mountain* (theoretically banned) or St. Augustine's treatise on "The Form as Structure."

Reading these books was one of the rules she had imposed on herself in order to survive the six months of hard work without getting "choked with sand." "I drift from one day to the next," she noted, sitting on a tree trunk in the park during an afternoon coffee break in May 1941, "not sad, not particularly cheerful, always keeping to my self-imposed rules."

Early in June she was allowed to work at an outdoor assignment for the first time. It meant a bit of freedom, but at the same time, it was hard physical work. On June 3 she wrote to her sister Inge:

Dear Inge,

Today for the first time I was at my new outdoor station. You wouldn't believe what a lovely road greets me each day (of course on some days I may curse it): a daily hour-long bicycle ride through the woods, often uphill and downhill, through a softly rolling countryside. The sky plays a big part in this landscape; today it was brilliant. We had really warm weather—in the field it felt hot—the sky was full of clouds as far as the eye could see. All those clouds in the dark-blue sky would, I figured, soon gather into a thunderstorm. They did loom in a threatening cluster, offering a marvelous view beyond the fir treetops, but then they graciously passed us by.

My first rural job today was weeding between tiny poppy plants. As I crawled along my furrow for hours and hours, always bent over, mindful not to pull the wrong plants, and therefore bent double all the time, I was contemplating, the way any lazybones would, how this sort of chore could be done more efficiently from the very start (before the poppies are mature, we'll have to weed three or four more times). But then I laughed at my mental effort. Always the same story! Theory is a lovely furrow with nothing but poppy plants; practice is a furrow with a few poppy plants hidden among lots of weeds. We should become resigned to that and keep weeding diligently. . . .

Making Decisions Against Oneself

The open-air work among the peasants, though it involved hard labor, made life more pleasant. But conditions inside the camp didn't change. Sophie had to share a dormitory room with ten girls. The meals were poor, since all over Germany the food situation was worsening. The main dish was always potatoes in their jackets. At the peasants' homes she at least got fresh milk and homemade bread. Field work left imprints that called for ironic self-inspection. The blisters on her hands changed into calluses; the palms of her hands had broadened ungirlishly; and, she said, her measurements had increased. But since there was a war on, that did not matter. In the summer of 1941, a year after France had surrendered, she met a French prisoner of war, a factory hand, with whom she sawed wood for an entire day. The two discussed politics and the war and discovered that their views were none too different. One silver lining of those summer weeks was a weekend visit from her sister Inge and their friend Otl Aicher. Inge Aicher-Scholl:

Sophie knew that we were coming and had arranged everything with her group leader. But on Saturday afternoon when I arrived up at the RAD camp and asked the leader for permission to see my sister, she said, "Come back in thirty minutes." I did, and she said, "It can't be done now. Come back at six." I came back at six, and she said, "They are all having dinner now; come back when they are through." On this short visit I got a taste of the harassment Sophie had to bear all the time. At last, on our fourth try, we managed to get her out, found a nice restaurant, had supper together, and afterwards took a stroll in the overgrown park by the castle. Of course Sophie had to return to the camp for the night. The next morning we were allowed to see her again. We went out and had breakfast together.

In the middle of it we heard the radio news: German troops had marched into the Soviet Union. That was a monstrous moment, that Sunday, June 22, 1941. We could well imagine what it meant. By then we had amassed enough political imagination, so to speak, to get the picture.

But in spite of the shocking newscast, that Sunday turned into a beautiful day for us. The valley of the upper Danube is one of the loveliest spots in southern Germany. We walked in the woods near the Danube. At night Sophie had to return to the camp. We could not go with her. For Otl, and me too, parting was sorrowful and depressing, like the end of a hospital visit. It is hard to leave behind someone you love.

During her labor service, Sophie often thought of a line

from a Goethe poem frequently quoted by her father: "Braving all powers, Holding your own." Sometimes their father would just call out, "Braving!" and the family knew what he meant. To Sophie it meant: Be tough on yourself; make decisions against yourself. Again and again she had to command herself to be tough. We can sense the bitterness in her letters. In August 1941 she noted that her brother Werner had been driven off course, into France, by the war; that her friend Fritz Hartnagle was with a tank unit in Russia, "far up front"; that the mail connection to him worked poorly, and that she herself was condemned to wait, strapped in the RAD straitjacket. "I believe that now the war is having its full effect in every regard." Late in August 1941 she was to be through with her RAD service, and she could hardly wait to shake off this yoke at long last.

Questioning About God

Sophie's anticipation of a reasonably normal life was dampened once again when she heard on the radio that prospective university students would first have to complete, right after finishing their labor service, another six months of community service called War Auxiliary Service. The news struck her like a sledgehammer, but she quickly recovered. The important thing was that she would soon leave the Krauchenwies camp. By early October she had reported for her new job—kindergarten teacher in a nursery school in Blumberg, a small town near the Swiss border. It still meant hard work, but at least she could move around more freely. And also, at long last she would see Fritz Hartnagel again. He had been called back from Russia to Weimar to organize a special unit for the North African campaign. That winter of 1941–42 they frequently met on weekends in Freiburg. They had many debates. Sophie sensed that her friend was changing, that he had attained greater spiritual security. In these discussions she often brought up religious themes. She felt they were closely knitted to political issues. Inge Aicher-Scholl reports:

It is difficult to describe Sophie's religious development, because the problems young people faced at that time were so different from today's. For Sophie, religion meant an intensive search for the meaning of her life, and for the meaning and purpose of history.

Like any adolescent, she had to arrive at her own personal insights. In the process of realizing yourself, you question the child's faith you grew up with, and you approach issues by reasoning. Your life plans start responding to the person you are. You discover freedom, but you also discover doubt about ways and means. That is why many people end up abandoning the search. With a sigh of relief they leave religion behind, and surrender to the ways society says they ought to believe. At this very point, Sophie renewed her reflections and her searching. The way society wanted her to behave had become too suspect.

But what was it life wanted her to do? She sensed that God was very much relevant to her freedom, that in fact he was challenging it. That freedom became more and more meaningful to her. In those years of total bondage, questioning about God opened her eyes to the surrounding world. There was no innermost preoccupation for her that would have allowed her to withdraw into her private soul to survive the catastrophe of the Third Reich and its war. The smallest step taken in daily life required a decision for freedom and permitted no retreat, no matter how tempting a retreat.

Her close relationship with nature was evidence to

Sophie that behind all living things there must be a creative force at work. But there was more. God was your insight into yourself. He was the only mirror in which you could see and understand yourself with any clarity. At that time He was the true essence of truth for us, the personal essence of personality, the essence of beauty. He was the quintessence of existence, life's victory over death and destruction.

Seeing this invisible force was one thing. The step that led to belief in a personal God, to whom you can say "thou" and who loves you—that step was almost too much to ask, almost too great an adventure. Such a decision took time. In a letter to Lisa Remppis, Sophie wrote:

Isn't it a tremendous enigma and, if we know the reason, almost frightening, that everything is so beautiful? In spite of all the terrible things that are going on. A great unknown has burst into my simple enjoyment of things beautiful, a faint vision of their creator, whom the innocent, created beings glorify with their beauty. Only man can be ugly. Being endowed with free will, he can seclude himself from the glorification. These days one might often think that man would manage to drown out this song of praise with his roaring cannons, with swearing and blaspheming. And yet— this dawned on me last spring—he cannot. And I will try to take the victors' side.

Ready to Travel and Full of Expectation—
Taking Leave of Ulm

Christmas 1941 marked half-time, so to speak, in Sophie Scholl's War Auxiliary Service. For the first time in many months she could unwind a bit after working in the nursery school to the brink of exhaustion. As a nursery school teacher she not only had to take care of the children, but had to be a cleaning woman as well. "This morning I scrubbed 150 chairs and 20 tables," she noted in one letter, and that was just a small part of the daily chores. After the Christmas and New Year's holidays she expected "an uncomfortable three months," since the Blumberg nursery school was to be headed by a new, "one-hundred-and-fifty-percent leader." But this too passed. In the end she found it hard to part from the children, for the girls especially were very fond of her. She realized that she had grown into an experienced kindergarten teacher.

Late in March 1942 she came back to Ulm. At first she found it difficult to readjust to family life after being alone and left to her own resources. She helped around the house and in her father's office and, as before, went on outings. Then, early in May, there was another separation from parents and sisters. Two long years after she had

96

graduated from high school, she was finally going to start on her philosophy and biology studies. In her book *The White Rose,* Inge describes her sister's farewell:

It was on the eve of Sophie's twenty-first birthday. "I can hardly believe that tomorrow I'm starting my studies," she had told her mother. Our mother was ironing Sophie's blouses in the hallway. On the floor lay an open suitcase with clothes and fresh linen and all the thousands of odds and ends Sophie would need in her new student household. Next to that stood a bag containing a crisp brown, fragrant cake. Sophie bent down and sniffed at it, and discovered a bottle of wine hidden next to it. . . .

I can still see her, my sister, standing there the next morning, ready to travel and full of expectation. A yellow daisy taken from her birthday table at her temple, she looked lovely with her dark brown hair, smooth and shiny, falling to her shoulders. She looked upon the world with her big, dark eyes questioning yet with lively sympathy. Her face was still very childlike and delicate.

97

On the Train, in Class, in the Backyard— Living with Fear

"How Do I Know if I'll Still Be Alive Tomorrow Morning?"

A New Beginning in Munich
Or, "Tonight You'll Get to Meet My Friends"

On May 9, 1942, Sophie took the train to go the 95 miles from Ulm to Munich. She could not know that this was to be her last birthday. Curious and eager, she anticipated Munich, where a new phase of her life was to begin. On arriving at the central railway station, she at once sought out her brother Hans. Anticipation turned into spontaneous joy. In this city there would be no need to feel lonely—that much was certain. She shared almost all of Hans' interests, and for years she had wished to be near her "big brother." He took her to his student lodgings. "Tonight you'll get to meet my friends, " he said.

They celebrated Sophie's birthday in Hans' room, relishing the wine and cake she had brought from Ulm, and they made Hans' sister feel as if she had always belonged to their group. Over the next several days and weeks she got to know her brother's friends better. Most of them were students who, like Hans, went to medical school. They also belonged to a students' unit and had to attend regular military drills. Chances were that the unit would be ordered to the front at any time.

Hans Scholl's closest friends were Alexander Schmorell, known as Schurik or Alex, Christoph (Christl) Probst, and

Willi Graf. Schmorell was the son of a Russian woman and a distinguished Munich physician. He went to medical school to please his father rather than because he felt a calling to medicine. Later, he and Sophie hired a model for their drawing and clay-modeling sessions. Christl Probst came from a family of Bavarian scholars. Sophie admired his intellectual proficiency and all-round education. "He has a good influence on Hans," she once wrote. Both he and Willi Graf may have been especially close to her in their theological and philosophical thinking. Willi had been born in Saarbrücken and was an active member of *Neu-Deutschland* (ND), a Roman Catholic youth league that had long been outlawed. In 1937 he had been rounded up in the same wave of arrests as Hans and Werner Scholl.

From the very first day, Sophie felt comfortable in their company. In this group, friendship didn't imply possessive claims. Their uncomplicated camaraderie, their interest in art, literature, and music, their enraptured love for nature, fit her own image of life.

Moreover, quite early on she came into close contact with a man who greatly influenced her brother and his friends, Professor Carl Muth, seventy-five years old. He had been editor-in-chief of *Hochland*, a literary-philosophical magazine banned by the Nazis but highly respected among progressive German Catholics. Between April 1933 and June 1941 it had contrived not to mention Hitler's name one single time.

At the time, Hans was arranging Professor Muth's ex-

tensive library. In return, and for friendship's sake, Muth gave Sophie, who had not found a place to stay yet, a room in his house in Solln near Munich. Sophie reciprocated for this hospitality every chance she had. On outings with her brother and his friends, she would remember to ferret out food for the professor. He was in poor health, and food was getting ever more scarce. If she could not hunt up something for him, she would write home. In her letter of June 6, 1942, she tells her parents and her two sisters:

He is not well. Current events are very hard on him, and our wartime nutrition is not exactly helping his general health. Couldn't you get a few pounds of white flour for him? That is what he misses especially. He cannot eat black bread. And trout, as soon as possible. Such things may seem petty, but to a large extent his health depends on them.

Most of the time these requests were promptly fulfilled. Supplies were more readily available in Ulm than in the big city of Munich.

The same letter continues:

The night before last, [the author] Sigismund von Radecki, encouraged by Hans, read some essays, poems, and translations to an audience of about twenty people. He reads altogether brilliantly, with huge gestures, acting out whatever he reads. Did we laugh! He used to be an actor, not a bad one, I'm sure. Afterward, he and the four of us continued the meeting in my room. Unfortunately, he will be out of town for three months, but after that he is ready to join us in all sorts of things.

Listening to lectures like the one described here and going to the theater and to concerts gave Sophie great pleasure. She never could get enough of them. She did have some trouble, at first, with the debates, which often went on into the late hours and were interspersed with foreign words and special technical terms. So many things were rushing in upon her that she felt out of her depth. In discussions like these she mostly just listened and rarely contributed remarks of her own.

There were some women students who belonged to the circle of friends and helped her find her way at the university, in particular Traute Lafrenz, a medical student from Hamburg, and Katharina Schüdderkopf, who was majoring in philosophy. They met not only at Hans' apartment, but also in town, in the few restaurants where they could still get food and wine for just a few ration coupons.

The White Rose
Or, We Have to Do Something

Munich, "the city of the Movement," where Hitler had tried to putsch his way to power as early as 1924, was the secret capital of National-Socialist Germany. Its university was among the richest in tradition—and among the most reactionary. Here, after the Berlin book-burning of March 1933, the Bavarian Minister of Education and Art, Hans Schemm, had staged another book-burning and, helped by professors and the National Socialist Students' League, "consigned to the flames" the works of writers banned in Nazi Germany, among them many whom Sophie and Hans Scholl and their Munich friends revered: Thomas and Heinrich Mann, Erich Kästner, Stefan Zweig, Franz Werfel, Bertolt Brecht, and Erich Maria Remarque. Munich's Maximilian University was to be a spiritual stronghold of National Socialism. Its president, Professor Walther Wüst, a high-ranking SS man, would see to that.

It was not by accident that in the summer of 1941, students at this very university began discussing what chances there were of resisting the dictator in Berlin and his many henchmen and surrogates all over Germany. Wherever reaction is strongest, opposition is bound to arise. By the spring of 1942 the group around Hans Scholl

had become convinced that there had been enough talk, and that the time for action had come. The Munich architect Manfred Eickemeyer, who was often in Poland and the Soviet Union on business, had told the students of mass deportations and mass shootings in the occupied areas. Hans had worked in army hospitals in conquered France and had seen the suffering the Nazis imposed on people. For those willing to listen, the word began getting around that Jews and handicapped people were being brutally exterminated.

What are we waiting for? the students wondered. The time for resistance had come. The only question left was how. They decided to issue leaflets calling for resistance to Hitler. Inge Aicher-Scholl recalls:

I think it is characteristic of the Munich students, choosing leafleting with its paper-thin chance of mobilizing passive resistance, because of its telegraphic style methods of enlightenment. They could have chosen to throw bombs, but that would have been at the cost of human lives. It's true that both Sophie and Hans would have endorsed tyrannicide—Hans, as we know, had entrenched himself for days in a Munich convent library to study the subject.

When they appealed to the populace to offer resistance, they did not intend violent liberation, even though some words, especially in the last leaflets, might seem to imply that. What they had in mind was that every in-

dividual and every group should do the utmost to achieve change, to have the regime gradually lose the ground under its feet, to make its ground porous, to turn the population against the dictator. The students collected dried white bread to send via go-betweens to concentration camp prisoners; they helped support the families of those prisoners; they refused to prolong Hitler's war by donating to the Nazi "Winter Aid" clothing drive that was to benefit German soldiers in Russia; they showed human understanding for prisoners of war and foreign workers. Examples for small-scale resistance, practical and tangible, and potentially contagious.

Their Christian faith constituted a significant motivation for what they were doing. As existentialism was the philosophy of French resistance, we had a Christian existentialism, strongly influenced by Sören Kierkegaard and [the Catholic philosopher] Theodor Haecker. The church hierarchy had been compromised by its initial alliance with National Socialism, and it kept quiet during those years. But countless Christians had gone underground, some of them into the resistance. Carl Muth and Theodor Haecker offered access to a liberating Christianity. As for the rational element of this existentialism, our view was: "Only when reasoning is at its wit's end, only then may we believe. Faith starts where reason has reached its limit." For Sophie of all people, it would have been difficult if not impossible to relinquish her reason even for a moment.

110

Their basic Christian attitude immensely helped the White Rose people to stop talking about resistance and start acting. Suddenly they saw one thing clearly. Being against is not enough. We have to *do* something. There is an enormous stone wall of impossibility, and our job is to discover minute possibilities that we can chip or blast out of the wall. Finding possibilities, even on the smallest scale, was extremely important for my sister Sophie. The passage from the Epistle of James, "But be ye doers of the word, and not hearers only," was an imperative for her.

It was this in the Christian religion that had finally made her take those last steps. The White Rose members were fully aware that in taking those steps they were risking their lives. There was no question about it, Sophie met with many a Christian inspiration. The way her Munich friends lived Christianity was more persuasive than the most sophisticated theological speculations. On coming home one day she told gleefully of a professor's plan to found an Erasmus club and to study the thoughts of the great humanist Erasmus of Rotterdam. She laughed and exclaimed, "As if at this moment we had nothing more important to do than found an Erasmus club!"

The Leaflets
Or, "The White Rose Will Not
Leave You in Peace."

Alexander Schmorell was the first to begin the practical preparations for printing leaflets. He had the biggest allowance, so he provided a typewriter, a mimeograph machine, stencils, and paper. Manfred Eickemeyer, the architect, let them use his studio in Leopoldstrasse. It was in a rear building giving onto a backyard, and hence most suitable. In May, June, and July of 1942 the first four leaflets were run off there—first a few hundred copies of each, later on more. Their masthead read: *"The Leaflets of the White Rose."* The origin of that name is not clear. Inge Scholl talked of it in a lecture she gave in 1964 in Amsterdam.

The exact meaning of this name can no longer be discovered. Perhaps the leaflets were being described as blank, anonymous sheets. Blank because they did not bear the stamp of parties or religious denominations. Anonymous in order to spare recipients the fear of becoming enmeshed in a dangerous organization. Blank, in a sense, is best described in one of the last letters my brother Hans wrote. 'When I used to cover a white sheet of paper with words, I was exhilarated by the joy of writing. Now, much of the time, this joy has disappeared.

113

Now I prefer a white sheet of paper, not for aesthetic reasons but because it carries no lie, no threadbare assertion; because a white sheet still holds potential power; because I can control myself and keep waiting for the day when writing will be a joy again.'

There are other possible interpretations of the name. Kurt Krüger-Lorenzen, for one, says in his 1938 book *German Expressions—And What Is Behind Them* that the rose "since ancient times has been the symbol of discretion, of secrecy. . . . When a rose was suspended from the ceiling at a rich Roman's banquet, that meant that the conversation would be off the record."

Possibly Hans Scholl knew B. Traven's novel *The White Rose*, in which Mexican peasants vainly defend their hacienda, La Rosa Blanca, against rapacious and murderous engineers and managers of an oil trust. But that, too, is only guesswork. What is true of the history of the name is true of some activities of the White Rose group itself. Many specific details are unknown because everything had to be done in utmost secrecy. They can be conjectured only with great caution and remain incomplete. This is particularly true for some of the following passages.

The first leaflet of the White Rose had been a close collaboration among Hans Scholl, Alexander Schmorell, and Christoph Probst. Its opening sentences read:

Nothing is more unworthy of a civilized nation than to be

115

ruled, unresisting, by an irresponsible gang of bosses given to sinister instincts. Can we deny that today every honest German is ashamed of his government? Which one of us can foretell the unspeakable shame that will be visited on us and our children when the scales fall from our eyes and the crimes, most horrible and infinitely beyond any measure, come to light? Is the German people, in its innermost soul, so corrupt and decayed? Will it, without lifting a finger, frivolously trusting questionable laws of history, surrender the most valuable thing man owns, that which raises him above all other creatures? Will the German people surrender free will, man's freedom to help put a spoke in the wheel of history and subordinate it to his own reason, his own decision? If Germans are so devoid of personal individuality, if they have become so irretrievably a mindless and craven mass— then, indeed then they deserve to perish.

In its later passages, the leaflet quotes Goethe and Schiller. It appeals to the German citizen's pride of culture. In the middle of the text there is a call for passive resistance, and finally a request: "Retype this page with as many carbon copies as possible, and pass it on."

When the leaflet emerged in Munich and its suburbs, it created a sensation. It had been a long time since anyone in Germany had dared say such things in public. The country was quiet as a graveyard—if you could disregard the bombing raids on the cities. And now such an exclamation bursting into the dull silence! Some who found it in their mailboxes took it to the police at once, that being their "lawful duty." Others disposed of it quickly after making sure that no one had been watching. But there were those

116

who screwed up their courage and followed the leaflet's request. They copied it in secret and passed it on. One of them said later, "Today no one will believe how happy we were to do something against the regime at long last."

The next three leaflets carried even more specific information. "The fact is that since the conquest of Poland 300,000 Jews have been bestially murdered in that country." The entire aristocratic youth of Poland had been annihilated. Polish girls had been deported to Norway and put into SS brothels. No one, the leaflets continued, who goes on watching these crimes without doing something about them can acquit himself of guilt.

Each one is guilty.

And, farther on,

The White Rose will not leave you in peace!

Nothing Was Certain

As the American author Richard Hansen said in his 1979 book *A Noble Treason*, the White Rose "had created a small island of resistance in an ocean of conformity." At first only Hans Scholl, Alexander Schmorell, Willi Graf, and Christoph Probst lived on this island. For resistance automatically means being isolated, keeping your friends at arm's length, living with fear. Including a friend in your plans imperils both. Their other student friends, therefore, at first did not know where the leaflets came from and who had written them.

It is not quite clear when and how Sophie was told of the leafleting actions. Possibly her brother meant to keep his sister out of it, to keep her out of harm's way. Nothing would be more natural. Fritz Hartnagel, though, recalls that as early as May 1942 Sophie asked him, without giving a reason, to get her a mimeograph machine, which he was unable to do. At any rate, it seems likely that soon after she arrived in Munich she took part in the group's deliberations and discussions on how to intensify their underground activities.

At Inge Scholl's request, in 1947 Traute Lafrenz wrote an account of how she learned about the White Rose.

118

Early in June 1942 my landlord's family got the first issue of *The White Rose* in the mail. From its contents, its syntax, and from well-known Goethe and Lao-tze quotations I could tell at once that it must have been written by "us," though I still wasn't sure that Hans himself had done it.

The next issue quoted a verse from Ecclesiastes that I had once given to Hans. Now I knew. I asked Hans about it. He said it was wrong to ask about the author, that such questions could only imperil such an author, that the number of immediate co-workers must be kept to a minimum, and that the less I knew the better for me. And that was that. I had been shown my place, and I accepted it. I saw to it that the leaflets were distributed.

119

But before further actions could be planned, that episode was over. All of a sudden the student company to which Hans and his friends belonged—all except Christl Probst—was ordered to Russia, to leave on July 22. On the eve of their departure, they met once more in Eickemeyer's studio to discuss ways of resistance after their return from Russia. Each of them sensed how dubious those reflections really were. Who, in the first place, would come back?

Sophie was sitting somewhat outside the circle and didn't say much. After a scant three months of living in Munich with her brother, here was the end.

The next morning they all gathered at the railway station. One of them took snapshots for remembrance. A few days later Sophie wrote to her friend Lisa Remppis.

Last week Hans went to Russia along with all the others who have become my friends over the past weeks and months. Every little word, every little gesture of that parting is still so very alive in me.

"Thoughts Are Free . . ."

After the summer term was over, there was nothing in
Munich to keep Sophie there. Anyway she was urgently
needed in Ulm, and for more than one reason. Her father
was scheduled to go on trial on August 3, 1942. It had
been expected for some time. Imprudently, in his office
and within hearing of a secretary, Robert Scholl had said
what he thought of the political situation and had called
Hitler "a great scourge of God." The secretary had no-
tified the Gestapo, and one early morning—the same as
once before, in November 1937—two men rang the doorbell and identified themselves as Gestapo officers. They
demanded to see Robert Scholl, asked him a few questions, searched the apartment, and eventually took him
and Inge away. (It was Inge's second arrest.)

They also seized a small attaché case full of papers,
among them a critical article on Napoleon worded in such
a way that the initiate could catch the parallels to Hitler.
But at headquarters, when the interrogating officer left
the room for a moment and his secretary pointedly looked
the other way, Inge took a chance and swiped the article
back. During her interrogation she was asked for the address of Rainer Maria Rilke. That made her feel a bit

safer. She could state truthfully that Rilke had been dead for several years. After the interrogation she was released.

Her father came home a few days later, but the Gestapo had told him in so many words that his "case" had not been settled yet. Early in August the "case" was tried before the Ulm Special Court. He was convicted of "malicious slander of the Führer" and sentenced to four months in prison. He surrendered to the court a few days later. His relatives could write him once every two weeks. He could write them once every four weeks. In this country of informers and surveillants, every detail was regulated most minutely. Nothing was left to chance.

On September 7 Sophie wrote her father in jail.

Dear Father: We all were very glad to get your letter, even though I had never worried that your good spirits might be broken by your so-called punishment. For I am convinced that this period is necessary for you, and that in a way we cannot yet grasp, it is the best thing that could happen to you—although I am never going to forget a single word of those who brought it about. Not as if I felt vengeful, but from quite a different viewpoint, which I'm sure you know.

Now that you are no longer here to keep us posted, I conscientiously listen to the news and often look at the map of Europe. I suppose you have received the Frankfurter Zeitung *and are keeping track of the most important developments. . . .*

Only good news from the front. Many friends to whom I wrote about you send regards. They are surrounding you with a wall of fond thoughts. All of them are helping build that wall. I know you can feel that you are not alone. Our thoughts tear down prison bars and prison walls. Thoughts—!

Your

Sophie.

[Sophie knew that her father would recognize the last sentence as part of a famous German song of freedom, and would complete the last phrase himself: "Thoughts are free!"] She had heard him quote the verse more than once.

"The smartest of his ladies," as Robert Scholl once jestingly called Sophie, had a courageous heart and a bright mind. Her father was in prison; her mother had a heart condition; both brothers were on active duty in Russia. Almost too much was asked of her, of her great courage and great endurance. All her strength was needed to maintain her brave defiance. Calling on that strength, on many a summer evening she went out with her flute to stand by the prison wall and play for her father the song that had become a symbol: *Die Gedanken sind frei.* [Thoughts are free. . . .]

In Blue Denims on the Assembly Line

Besides her father's trial, there had been another reason, literally a "compelling" one, for Sophie to return to Ulm. In spite of having done her labor service and war auxiliary service, she had to pay additional tribute to the Nazi state. She was assigned to an "armament job," meaning that for two months she had to work in an arms factory and so help maintain the flow of matériel to the front. What frightened her was not the hard physical labor required, but the fact that she personally would be contributing to prolonged senseless slaughter and death. Yet she didn't even try to get out of the assignment. She knew it would have been futile. She merely applied for a month's delay to help relieve her ill mother in her work, just for a little while. But the authorities refused even that.

Starting early in August she worked for eight weeks in a factory—an incisive experience for the twenty-one-year-old. The personnel included not only students but "slave labor" from the Soviet Union. In her letter to Lisa Remppis of September 2, she described the alienation the workers suffered from.

My factory job is terrible. The mindless and lifeless labor, the empty mechanics, the tiny little piece of a fraction of

work with its sum total unknown, with its horrifying pur-
pose, is physically exhausting and even more so mentally.
Nor are the ceaseless clanging of the machines, the fright-
ening howl of the time-off siren, the degrading sight of
human beings subjected to the full power of the machine,
any help in strengthening my nerves. How beautiful, by
contrast, the labor of a farmer, a craftsman, even a street
sweeper! The one refreshing activity is cleaning the machine
on Saturday, scouring it till it shines. That's the only time
you have a purpose and a whole job to do, and its result
can be as thrilling as a housewife's sparkling-clean kitchen.

A charming Russian woman works next to me. I am
trying to apply what little Russian I know, and I have even
learned a few additional words, for instance siergy, *that is,*
earrings. These Russian women take a childlike delight in
jewelry. Almost all of them have pierced ears and have
bought cheap earrings. In other ways, too, they are much
more childlike than the German women workers, for in-
stance in their totally innocent and unsuspecting dealings
with Germans. A lovely, touching trait. When they are
brutally bawled out, they just don't understand it and laugh
merrily. Oh what a shame it would be if they, too, were to
catch distrust and utilitarianism from us, the "high-minded"
Europeans.

Feeling and Reasoning: Poles Apart
Or, Diary Dreams

Even after exhausting factory work, Sophie had time and strength left to give to her diary, which she had started writing a few years earlier. There are reflections on her existence, her feelings, moods, and dreams. The expressions she invents as she clothes her innermost life in words have—like many of her letters—an urgent beauty and a painter's density. In August 1942 her diary describes a dream.

I was on a walk with Hans and Schurik—I was in the middle, arm in arm with both of them, half walking, half skipping. The two would lift me and pull me along for a while. I was floating on air. Then Hans said, "I know a very simple proof that God is alive and at work, even in our time. You see, people need air to breathe, and as time goes on you would expect the entire sky to be polluted by their spent breath. But, so that people wouldn't run short of this nourishment for their blood, every once in a while God blows a mouthful of his breath into our world, and that breath permeates all our used-up air and renews it. This is how he does it": Here Hans raised his face to the gloomy, gloomy sky, took a deep breath, and pushed all that air out of his wide-open mouth. As his breath streamed forth, it was a pillar, radiant blue. The pillar grew taller and taller, way up into the sky. It pushed away the dirty

clouds, and there, ahead of us, above us and all around us, there was the purest, bluest sky. It was lovely.

In another diary passage, Sophie speaks of the dangers everyone was exposed to in Germany in the war year of 1942. She was aware that at any time she might be killed in an air raid, but she was not frightened. She wrote soberly:

Many people believe that our time is the end of time. All those terrible portents could seem to lend credence to such a belief. But isn't it an irrelevant one? Don't we all know, no matter in which times we live, that at a moment's notice God can call us to account? How do I know if tomorrow morning I'll still be alive? This very night a bomb could annihilate us all. And my guilt would not be any smaller than if I were to perish along with the earth and the stars.

In yet another passage Sophie describes her relationship with nature. She visualizes herself on a raft, standing tall, "enfolded by the wild, impetuous wind." The sun comes out and kisses her tenderly, and she wishes she could kiss it back. She wishes she could shout for joy "that I am so alone," and she senses great inner strength. It is an exuberant vision she draws in this diary passage, offering a remarkable contrast to her usual sober, sometimes almost cool, thoughts and reflections.

Erich Kuby, a Hamburg political writer, has persuasively explained this contradiction. In a long article on the White

Rose, published on February 21 and 22, 1953, the tenth anniversary of Hans and Sophie Scholl's execution, he writes:

Sophie Scholl, though younger, was more mature and more sober than her friends, who were generally older. In her school days a teacher once had called her frivolous, and at home she asked what that word meant. In this case, among other things, it had meant a misconception—though an easy-to-understand one—on the teacher's part. Sophie Scholl's reasoning was rational and would not be misled by her emotions. But neither did it harness her emotions. The two poles of clear logic and visionary sensitivity were much farther apart in her than in most other people.

We can discern these two poles in her letters to Fritz Hartnagel, whom she had not seen since the spring of 1942. Mail contact between the two had grown more and more difficult. Sophie did not even know whether her letters reached her friend. On October 7, 1942, the day her brother Hans came home, she wrote to Fritz:

Tonight Hans returns from Russia. Well, I suppose I should rejoice that he is with us once again, and I do rejoice. I visualize the time which we will have together in our little apartment, and which could well be very fruitful.

And yet my joy is not unclouded. The uncertainty we constantly live under, which prohibits any cheerful plan-

ning for tomorrow and casts a shadow on all the days to come, oppresses me night and day and really haunts me every single minute. Oh for a time when we don't have to tax our energies and our attention to the breaking point attending to things not worth moving a little finger for! Every word, before being spoken, is scrutinized from all sides lest even a shadow of ambiguity taint it. Confidence in other people must yield to suspicion and caution. It is so wearying and sometimes so discouraging.

But no, I refuse to let anything discourage me. Why, this nothingness cannot be my master when I own quite different things, inviolable joys. Thinking of them gives me strength, and I would like to shout an encouraging word to all who are depressed the way I am.

I have had no mail from you for so long that I'm getting worried. Have you by any chance been transferred? Judging from your past letters, that seems very unlikely. But if you are all right I will gladly wait. Also, perhaps some mail has gotten lost.

I wish I could once again hike through the woods or anywhere with you. But that is still in the far, though not unattainable, future. Meanwhile a letter must do for me, carrying many heartfelt thoughts from

Your

Sophie.

Money for the Underground

Early in October 1942 Hans Scholl, Alexander Schmorell, and Willi Graf returned to Munich. Not only had they come to know the breadth and the beauty of the Russian countryside, but with their own eyes they had witnessed all the misery of the war and the annihilation campaign waged in the occupied areas by the SS and parts of the army. In the article mentioned earlier, Erich Kuby writes about these experiences.

Right at the beginning, during the twelve days of their train ride to Russia, one of the friends became a central figure. Able to speak Russian, son of a German father and a Russian mother, and born in Russia, Alexander Schmorell now was coming back to Russia as to his second homeland. Known by his family and friends by the Russian name Schurik, he had never gone through a phase of enthusiasm for National Socialism. He was born with nothing less than a fanatical need for freedom and independence. He had a stubborn sense of fairness. He was an artist more than anything else and wanted to be a sculptor, going to medical school only to please his father. These qualities, together with his freewheeling temper, had—first in the labor service and later in the army—gotten him into many a scrape, from which his father, aided by understanding superiors, had to rescue him. His encounter with Russia affected him like a drug. Since he was fluent in Russian, he and his friends came in close touch with the Russian population. Like many other sensitive German soldiers, they were overwhelmed by the vastness of the Russian country and of its sky. At the same time they experienced the regime in one of its most terrible aspects. They saw the evil it did to the country and the abuse it inflicted on the "subhuman" Russians, whom Hans and his friends had come to love and respect.

They must have had a wild and daring time during these Russian months. Often they ran great risks when they opposed German violence being done to Russians, and court-martial proceedings brought against them were only barely quashed. Schmorell played the balalaika, and they all learned to appreciate vodka. After wriggling out of many a fix, they came to feel that nothing could happen to them. In this state of mind they returned to Munich, where the misery of war had been rising and would get even worse with the catastrophe of Stalingrad.

They had no more doubts: We must do our utmost to carry on the resistance. Sophie arrived in Munich with similar intentions. Her two months in the arms factory, and her father's imprisonment, had reinforced her deter-

mination to be active in the resistance. Robert Scholl meanwhile had been released—paroled from the rest of his sentence, but barred from going back to work. He would have had to look for a low-level, subordinate book-keeping job, hardly sufficient to support a big family, let alone send his children to the university. But things were to turn out differently.

During the weeks before Christmas, the students made new contacts and cautiously expanded the resistance group. Professor Kurt Huber, the book dealer Josef Soehngen, and the student Jürgen Wittenstein joined in. Professor Huber, whose philosophy classes Sophie regarded highly, soon played an important part in the White Rose. Josef Soehngen was another of the older friends and advisors with whom students could relax and let off steam. Also Soehngen, helped by the art historian Stepanov, took the first steps in making contact with the Italian resistance.

One weekend in November Hans Scholl and Alexander Schmorell went to Chemnitz to meet Falk Harnack, the brother of Arvid Harnack, who had been imprisoned as one of the leaders of the Red Orchestra (*Rote Kapelle*), a [communist] resistance organization. Through Falk Harnack they tried to get in touch with the men and women who later, on July 20, 1944, were to fail in their attempt to assassinate Hitler. Furthermore, the White Rose was to help build as many resistance cells as possible in other German universities. The cells were to start educational actions along the lines of the Munich group. Actually, by then a similar loose alliance existed in Hamburg. In November Traute Lafrenz went there for a few weeks and presented the White Rose's plans to that student opposition group. There was avid interest in Traute's proposals and suggestions, and soon actual underground work was started.

First of all, though, the Munich students needed money to get new mimeograph machines, typewriters, and paper. Sophie asked for, and got from her friend Fritz Hartnagel, 1,000 marks "for a worthy purpose." Early in December 1942 Hans and Sophie Scholl went to Stuttgart, where Hans conferred with a tax consultant, Eugen Grimminger. Grimminger had a Jewish wife and, as a friend, had seen to Robert Scholl's office while Scholl was doing his time. Sophie, meanwhile, went to see Susanne Zeller, her friend from the Fröbel Seminary, who was now a music student. Many years later, in her letter to Inge mentioned earlier (August 27, 1979), Susanne described Sophie's visit.

Sophie came to see me in Stuttgart while Hans was at Grimminger's asking for money. She suggested that I come to a meeting in Eickemeyer's studio. But since the music college was performing a Haydn oratorio and there were very few cellists besides me, I couldn't come. Sophie hinted at leafleting actions. We went out to meet Hans on Calwer Street, and on the way there she said, "If Hitler were to come toward me right now and I had a gun, I would shoot him. If the men won't do it, well, then a woman will have to." I envied her her positive commitment, since I myself suffered from doubts, and I said, "Well, then we'd have Himmler, and after him plenty of others." She replied, "One has to *do* something—or else be guilty." Those were the last important words we exchanged. We met Hans in the café and had cherry cake. Hans was euphoric. He had succeeded; he had found a sympathizer in Grimminger. He was convinced that the nation would arise if given a shove.

Printing the leaflets and distributing them involved great effort and great dangers. Whenever there was an air raid, the students had to interrupt their work and lug the mimeograph into the basement of the studio or of Soehngen's bookstore, where it was hidden under cardboard boxes. To work the mimeograph you didn't just push a button but hand cranked it. The students took turns cranking. Sophie joined in the work most of the time. She got stencils and paper—with great caution. Someone might become suspicious if she patronized the same store. At one time Traute Lafrenz went all the way to Vienna just to hunt up a new mimeograph in her uncle's wholesale office-equipment shop.

Sophie and her friends spent many nights in the studio. She barely had time to write letters, because the leaflets had to be distributed as widely as possible, not only in Munich. Acting as couriers, the students themselves carried them to other cities. With a tightly packed old school

136

bag or backpack, Sophie would shuttle between Augsburg, Stuttgart, and Ulm. Had a Gestapo officer checked her bag, she would have been arrested on the spot. To lessen the danger, the courier would leave the bag or backpack in one train compartment at the beginning of the trip, sit in another compartment, and a few minutes before arrival time, pick up the luggage.

Soon the White Rose leaflets appeared in many German cities: Frankfurt, Berlin, Hamburg, Freiburg, Saarbrücken, even in Salzburg and Vienna. A few copies even turned up abroad: in Norway, England, and Sweden. The Munich Gestapo was in a state of extreme alarm. It set up a special commission for one purpose: to search out the resistance group.

The group's activities went on into the second half of December 1942. When the members parted for the Christmas recess, they firmly resolved to make good use of that time and enlist new helpers and comrades-in-arms among friends and acquaintances.

Fear Was Part of Everyday Life

Hans and Sophie Scholl spent the Christmas holidays in Ulm. Talking with his sister Inge, Hans tried to give her a hint about their Munich resistance activities. He told her, showing great sympathy, that only recently fourteen Communist and Social-Democratic resistance fighters had been executed in Mannheim. "It is high time that Christians, too, start doing something. Christians have to set up a visible sign of resistance. When we are asked at the end of the war, 'What did you do?' shall we stand there empty-handed?" He realized that Inge was getting panicky and that he had better drop his suggestions. Inge asked him, "Why *us*? The track leading to our house is beaten enough as it is. Can't we leave it to others who are less well known to the Gestapo?" Hans changed the subject. He would not and must not more gravely endanger his parents and his brother and sisters, endanger their very lives.

Inge occasionally visited Sophie and Hans in Munich, but she had no clear idea of what exactly was going on. She knew their attitude. She knew that articles critical of the regime were circulating. Once in a while a passing word registered with her that only afterward was to fit into a context. Looking back, she feels almost relieved that she did not see the full extent of the looming danger. Mere suggestions were enough to provoke, again and again, helpless dread.

One day my sister, coming home from Munich, brought one of the White Rose leaflets. She handed it to father and watched him with anxious eyes. Wouldn't he be glad to see a sign of resistance? He was glad indeed, but suddenly he asked, "Sophie, I do hope you people have nothing to do with this?" Switching tracks quickly, she acted indignant. "How can you even think of such a thing? Sure there is fermentation all over Munich. But people like us don't get involved in those things." That set his mind at rest.

White Rose leaflets appeared in Ulm mailboxes. One day the mother of a student friend came to our house, all aflutter, a leaflet in her trembling hand, to ask if we knew where this sheet came from and if Hans and Sophie had had anything to do with it. I replied, almost furious, "How can you have such suspicions?" The woman left, pacified, after first asking what she ought to do about the leaflet—would she have to go to the police? To her relief, I took it and threw it down the drain.

Sophie's behavior, in retrospect, gave a clue to what was going on in Munich. Our parents' house was her rightful place to relax, and she thoroughly enjoyed the days she spent at home. It did her good to be cared for by Mother, with Father in the background to provide security and calm amid all the dangers. She once said that the ninety-five miles from Ulm to Munich changed a cheerful, relaxed, carefree child into a totally grown-up adult every time. Yet I can well imagine that Sophie would have liked to shake off the burden of growing up and the challenge of resistance. Both of them, Hans and Sophie, loved life and would have liked to stay a bit longer on the beautiful island of youth. It was not foolhardiness that banished them from their island, nor was it idealism. It was just the opposite; the evolution from idealism to reality—a very ill-fitting reality, to be sure.

The Stone Is Beginning to Roll

In early January 1943 Sophie and Hans Scholl returned to Munich. Since November, Sophie had been living at 13 Franz-Joseph-Strasse, in a room right next to her brother's. So the two of them were able to plan and do many things together. Indeed they had a lot to discuss. Issuing a new leaflet and distributing it in as many big cities as possible called for extensive preparations and security measures.

The new leaflet was entitled: An Appeal to All Germans! Its first sentence read:

> The war is approaching its certain end.

And a few lines farther down:

> Hitler cannot win the war—He can only prolong it.

The group had long been convinced of that. But this leaflet added a few new points. It spoke of "power-hungry imperialism," of a "reasonable socialism," a "federalist Germany." These passages reflected the group's discussions. The resistance of the White Rose had grown more resolute and more radical, and in some ways more political. Their discussions often dealt with the question: What should be done after the Hitler dictatorship has been overthrown?

Working hard, Alexander Schmorell, Willi Graf, and Hans and Sophie Scholl ran off several thousand copies of the new leaflet. They had to ensure that its distribution would not reveal its Munich origins. Alexander Schmorell took the train to Salzburg; Jürgen Wittenstein and Helmut Hartert organized the Berlin distribution; Sophie Scholl again covered Augsburg, Stuttgart, and Ulm. The envelopes had been addressed, stuffed, and stamped in Munich. Sophie took the train to Augsburg and put them into several different mailboxes. Then she went on to Ulm, where she had arranged to meet the high school student Hans Hirzel, her friend Susanne's brother. He took a stack of leaflets to Stuttgart.

Willi Graf kept a diary about those turbulent January days. Among other things he noted:

january 11, 1943—in the evening we again visit in the studio. it is the eve of our host's departure. there is much talking, and many a good idea is born. geyer, the painter, is here in munich for a few days.

january 13, 1943—the days pass with unusual haste. visited hans, and again in the evening. we are indeed starting our work; the stone is beginning to roll.

The stone did indeed begin to roll. With the expanding radius of action, the risks also grew. But all the friends, again and again, returned safely from their perilous travels.

An Insolent Leader
Or, "Don't Go to University, Give the Führer a Child!"

In the second part of January, morale rapidly deteriorated at Munich University. For days on end, the students discussed an incident that had occurred on January 13, the day the university celebrated its 470th anniversary. During a commemorative assembly in the German Museum, the city's Nazi leader, Paul Giesler, called upon the women students to "give the Führer a child" rather than hang around at the university. As for the less pretty girls, Giesler promised to assign each of them one of his adjutants, "and I can promise each one a thoroughly enjoyable experience" (William L. Shirer, *The Rise and Fall of the Third Reich*).

Furious at this insult, some women students stood up and angrily rushed to the exit. On Giesler's orders, SS men arrested them. Within minutes, the fury of the male students exploded. They chanted demands for their co-students' release. Some crowded up to the lectern, pulled the Nazi student leader down, beat him up, and declared that they would keep him as a hostage until the women students had been released. A police squad, summoned by telephone, restored order, and for the moment settled the dispute in favor of Giesler.

144

A few days later—the women students were released—there was another assembly. Giesler again uttered wild threats, but this time he apologized for his speech. The people who had protested, among them White Rose members, realized that they were no longer powerless.

Up till January 13, 1943, there had been no open rebellion at a student assembly in Munich. After that day the Gestapo redoubled its efforts to exterminate the spreading resistance germ. The Special Commission officers had vague leads on some suspect persons, but nothing specific. With leaflets now appearing in so many different cities, they became more and more nervous.

The Munich students were well aware of the rising danger. More than ever before, the group found themselves in situations that urged them on to yet other activities—and made them make mistakes. Once in a while the machinery for printing leaflets was left lying exposed. Putting it away at once, after each use, was a matter of absolute necessity but was neglected at times because of fatigue. It would be easy to blame Sophie and Hans Scholl and the others for thoughtlessness or carelessness. Unlike the Communists, these students lacked tight organization [and decades of experience]. They had hardly even heard about underground work before they started experimenting with their own, and they had to learn and improvise practically everything that could make an action successful.

Moreover, all that vast amount of work had to be restricted to a very small group of people. Every additional hand might increase the risk. Manfred Eickemeyer, the architect, later on testified to the great caution and thoroughness Hans Scholl, for one, used whenever new people were to be introduced into the discussions. No one, Eickemeyer said, was admitted without having his character and political convictions painstakingly examined. There can be no question of thoughtlessness. There was great caution; there was shrewdness and imagination, and there were, after all, physical limits set to all their activities.

Writing FREEDOM in Tar Paint
Or: "The Night Is a Friend of the Free"

Often after a successful leafleting action, there would be a phase of inner emptiness even harder to bear than the preceding tension. Sophie felt the gap very strongly. In her last diary entry, January 13, she wrote:

As soon as I am alone, sadness represses any wish to do anything. If I do pick up a book, it's not that I'm interested but as if someone else were reading it. There is only one thing that helps me get over this horrible state. I would a thousand times rather have the worst pain, even if it were mere physical pain, than feel so empty and becalmed.

In the few letters she wrote in January, she also complained about this despondency. On January 19 she wrote Otl Aicher of minor frictions she was having with herself, "My thoughts leap hither and thither. I cannot control them." Only from her parents did she conceal how badly out of joint her soul was. On January 30 she wrote her mother to send her a white tablecloth and some floor wax, the next time Wilhelm Geyer came to Munich. Her floor needed a better appearance, for a change.

147

Elisabeth Scholl who came to visit Hans and Sophie around that time remembers:

For about ten days, until February 5, I stayed with Hans and Sophie in the Munich house at 13 Franz-Joseph-Strasse. I didn't notice the slightest trace of any activities. I offered to help give their apartment a thorough cleaning. Even though I didn't come across any suspicious-looking objects, I couldn't understand why Sophie got so upset about a military train pass from Saarbrücken that Alex had left lying around. She was angry about such "care-lessness."

There was a Russian blouse of Alex Schmorell's in the apartment. Sophie said, half jokingly, "He wears it occasionally when he does Russian dances with some Russian working men and women in a basement room. It gives him the feeling he's in Russia."

Another day Christl Probst, passing through Munich, dropped in. I found it strange that in spite of his short stay—only an hour and a half—he took off his uniform and changed into civilian clothes and he and Hans withdrew into Hans's room. Afterwards we had tea together and spoke about Christl's wife, who had just had her third child and was in the hospital with childbed fever.

One evening Hans went out with Alex Schmorell—to the women's hospital, they said. A moment later Willi Graf came up. When I told him they had gone to the women's hospital, he laughed and said they wouldn't go there without him. That evening, as we walked in the English Garden, Sophie seemed very nervous to me. She said one ought to do something, for instance, write on walls. I said, "I have a pencil in my pocket." Sophie: "It has to be done with tar-based paint." I: "But that's insanely dangerous." Sophie, evasively: "The night is a friend of the free."

When we had returned to the apartment, Hans called up and said, "Go and get a bottle of wine. I've found fifty marks in my pocket." There was a black-market dealer in the building, and for special occasions one could pick up a bottle of wine from him at 20 marks. Soon Hans, Alex, and Willi came back, their minds at ease, and we had a relaxed and pleasant evening.

Next morning I went with Sophie and Hans to the university to attend Professor Huber's class on Leibniz. There was a big crowd of students by the university entrance staring at the stone wall. As we came closer we saw the word FREEDOM printed in black paint in three-foot-high letters. Several cleaning women were busily trying to scrub off the writing. An older student said to Sophie, "Those bastards!" Hans urged us to walk on—"We don't want to be conspicuous." As we left, Sophie said to me under her breath, "They have a long scrub ahead of them; that's tar paint."

That same morning Traute Lafrenz was also at the university. She observed Hans coming through the entrance.

149

I saw Hans coming toward me from the other side . . . taking long strides, a bit stooped (his posture had been bad for some time). He passed by the . . . crowd, his face wide awake with a high-spirited little smile. As we went on into the university, past legions of cleaning women wielding brooms, brushes, and buckets to scrub the writing off the wall, that smile expanded. An excited student ran up to him, "Have you seen it?" And Hans, laughing out loud, "No, what's the matter?" At that moment I started being terribly afraid for him.

"I Hope You Are Very Well"

On February 3, 1943, the radio newcast reported an event that changed a lot of things. The battle of Stalingrad was over. The German army had suffered its most devastating defeat ever. It was never to recover from it. After that, the communication between Sophie and Fritz, exchanging letters, grew even more difficult and fragile. Fritz Hartnagel, the army officer in the forefront of the battle; Sophie Scholl, the philosophy and biology student fighting as a war resister—yet this paradox did not affect their friendship. Not knowing whether her letters would ever reach him, Sophie kept on sending them to Russia. She told him about her daily life and her circle of acquaintances, and she never stopped worrying about her friend: "I hope you are well, that the din and misery of war will not throw you off your straight road."

Early in February she wrote Fritz that Otl Aicher was home on leave and that he had sculpted her. "Now my hands are eager to do as he did. I'm looking forward to it. Pen and pencil are much too impatient to take hold of a face. Besides, they lack the feeling of certainty that I get on handling the clay, an almost seductive certainty."

On February 16 she wrote Fritz what was to be her last

letter. She wrote about her stay at home in Ulm, of her parents and of the two worlds that for her separated Munich from Ulm.

Dear Fritz!

Just a short greeting before I run off to my classes. I believe I wrote you that I had been at home for ten days to help out. Although I don't get much of a chance to do my own things, that kind of stay always does me good, if only because my father is so delighted when I come home and surprised when I leave, and my mother is so concerned about a thousand little things. To me this love, which I get so free of charge, is something marvelous, one of the most beautiful things given to me.

My trip back, the ninety-five miles between Ulm and Munich, transforms me so rapidly that I'm surprised myself. From a harmless, exuberant child I turn into a grown-up with only myself to rely on. But this independence is good for me, even though sometimes I feel sorry for myself in being so alone. After all, I have been spoiled by people. I feel truly safe and at peace, for I sense an unselfish love—and that is comparatively rare.

The Last Leaflet

Since the battle of Stalingrad, the White Rose members knew that time was on their side. They began to plan their next leaflet at once, since it was a time when hope ran high Hitler would fall. It was to be the last leaflet of the White Rose.

Fellow Students!
The men at Stalingrad have perished. Our shaken nation has witnessed the spectacle of three hundred thirty thousand German men being driven into death and destruction by our World War corporal's brilliant strategy—senselessly, irresponsibly. [Only ninety thousand survived and surrendered.] Führer, we thank you!

There is great ferment in the German nation: Are we to continue to trust an amateur with the fate of our armies? Are we to sacrifice the rest of German youth to the basest power plays of a party clique? Never again! The day of reckoning has come, the day when German youth must settle accounts with the most despicable tyranny our people have ever endured. In the name of the German people we demand that Adolf Hitler's state give back to us our personal freedom, the most precious treasure ever owned by the German people, most wretchedly swindled from us.

We have grown up in a state where all free expression has

been ruthlessly gagged. In the most fertile, young years of our lives Hitler Youth, SA, and SS have endeavored to standardize, condition, and anesthetize us. "Philosophical education" they called their contemptible method of suffocating nascent free thought in a fog of empty phrases. An inconceivably diabolic and at the same time narrow-minded leader-selection program trains future party leaders to become godless, shameless, unscrupulous exploiters and killers, blindly and stupidly following their Führer. We, the so-called brain workers, would suit this new ruling caste just fine as its bullyboys. Student leaders and aspiring national leaders castigate war veterans as if they were schoolboys. National leaders, joking lewdly, assail women students' honor. At Munich University, German women students made a fitting, dignified reply to that defilement of their honor. German male students stood by their female colleagues, and stood firm. . . . This was only the first step taken to gain back our free self-determination. No spiritual values can be created without that freedom. We owe thanks to our brave comrades, both women and men, who have set us such a glowing example!

There is only one watchword for us: Fight the Party! Get out of the Party organizations where they silence you with "No politics!" Get out of the lecture rooms of SS leaders and SS chief leaders and Party toadies! We are committed to true science and genuine freedom of thought! Neither by threats nor by shutting down our universities can they frighten us. Every last one of us must fight for our future, for our freedom and honor in a state that must be aware of its moral responsibility.

Freedom and honor! For ten long years Hitler and his lackies have drained, vulgarized, and distorted those two glorious German words ad nauseam, the way only amateurs can when they cast the highest values of a nation before swine. For ten long years, destroying all material and spiritual freedom and all the

155

moral substance of the German nation, they have blatantly shown how little freedom and honor mean to them. Even the most simple-minded German had his eyes opened by the terrible bloodbath that they, in the name of the German nation's freedom and honor, have inflicted on all of Europe and still inflict every day. The German name will remain disgraced forever unless German youth rises and, avenging and atoning at the same time, smashes its tormentors and builds a new spiritual Europe.

Students! The German nation is watching us! As in [the] 1813 [War of Liberation] it expected the power of the spirit to break the Napoleonic terror, so in 1943 it expects that same spirit to break the National Socialist terror. The battles of the Berezina River and Stalingrad blaze in the East. The Stalingrad dead adjure us!

"Bravely on, students! The beacons are aflame!" Our nation sounds the march against National Socialism's enslavement of Europe. There will be newly impassioned faith in freedom and honor.

When the leaflets had been run off, Hans and Sophie Scholl assumed responsibility for personally distributing them at Munich University.

156

Life in Prison

"I Would Do Everything Again, Exactly the Same Way."

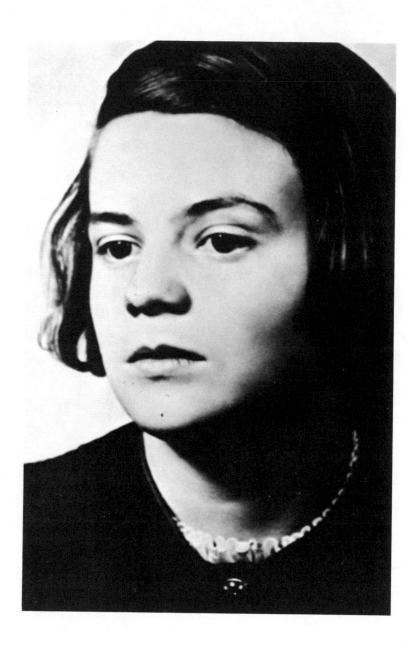

"You Are Under Arrest"
February 18, 1943

February 18 was a Thursday. From early morning on, the sun shone brightly and the weather was mild, almost like early spring. Sophie and Hans had gotten up at their usual hour, had breakfast together, and went out around ten o'clock. Traute Lafrenz and Willi Graf, having left their class a little early, were rushing to a seminar in the mental hospital when Sophie and Hans walked up to them carrying a valise. The four of them exchanged a few words and made a date for the afternoon. Sophie and Hans were in a hurry too and hastened to the university. Classes were conducted in the lecture halls, but stairways, window seats, and ledges were empty at that hour. So it was there that they scattered most of their leaflets, then rushed to the exit. Once outside, it occurred to them that they ought to empty their valise completely and distribute the few remaining leaflets. They dashed upstairs again and tossed them into the courtyard, just seconds before the lecture-hall doors opened.

Sophie and Hans headed toward the stairs but were stopped by the janitor, Jakob Schmid, a former mechanical engineer. He was agitated and grabbed them by their arms, yelling "You are under arrest!" several times.

Sophie and Hans were composed and resigned. The janitor took them to the building superintendent, who took them to the president, SS-Oberführer Professor Walther Wüst, who in turn called the Gestapo. The officers had the situation "under control" in no time. An eyewitness, Christa Meyer-Heidkamp, a student who knew Hans Scholl from Professor Huber's classes, recalls how it happened.

All exits [of the university] were barred. All students were ordered to assemble in the courtyard. Whoever had picked up a leaflet was to hand it to the man in charge of collecting them. We stood there waiting for two hours until finally Hans Scholl and his sister were led away in handcuffs. He looked at us once more, but nothing in his face showed that he knew us. He was well aware that any fellow student he knew could be suspect in the officers' eyes.

Brother and sister were interrogated by the Gestapo right there in the courtyard. They both stated calmly that they had nothing to do with the leaflets. They happened to be passing by when the janitor had unjustly seized them. After the brief questioning, the Gestapo tried to put the collected leaflets into the valise to see if they fit inside. They did.

160

They took Hans and Sophie to the Wittelsbach Palais, Gestapo headquarters, where the interrogation continued. One of the Gestapo officers, Robert Mohr, a former policeman in charge of the interrogation, conducted it in a reasonably businesslike manner. After a while, he grew doubtful whether he was in actual fact dealing with two members of the resistance group. Both of them, tenaciously and convincingly, stuck to their story: The case with the leaflets had nothing to do with them. But then they were confronted with evidence the Gestapo had found in their rooms at 13 Franz-Joseph-Strasse: several hundred new eight-pfennig postage stamps, an ominous piece of evidence which gravely incriminated the two defendants.

The following day, Friday, February 19, Christoph Probst was delivered into the Gestapo's hands. As on every Friday, he was to draw his soldier's pay in the office of the student company in Innsbruck. Instead he was ordered to report immediately to his commanding officer. The Gestapo henchmen were waiting; they arrested him, and led him away in handcuffs. Alexander Schmorell managed to escape but after wandering about for several days, he returned to Munich and was arrested there on February 24.

After the war Jakob Schmid, the janitor, was sentenced by the Americans to five years in a labor camp. Following his arrest he wrote an application for release, which was put into his file.

Request for release of the mechanical engineer Jakob Schmid. On May 11, 1945, I was arrested by the Americans and delivered to the Neudeck prison. I am in my sixtieth year now and never had anything to do with the courts. In the Scholl case, too, I never intended to have anything to do with the courts. I cannot understand why I, of all people, am being kept a prisoner, while my former superiors, whom I had to obey, are, I was sorry to learn, at liberty—and some of them have kept their old jobs.

Jakob Schmid never felt any pangs of conscience, either then or later. He was convinced that he had done his duty by keeping order at the university. At his trial he declared that he would have arrested the students [for littering] even if all they had tossed out had been sandwich wrappers.

The Code Word Arrived Too Late
Or, They Knew the Danger

Well before they were arrested on February 18, Hans and Sophie were in danger, and they seem to have been aware of it. Josef Soehngen, the book dealer, had seen Hans for the last time on February 16. They had discussed the leaflet and Hans' intention to personally distribute it at the university in the next few days. Soehngen urgently tried to persuade him that he had to remain anonymous. According to Soehngen:

Hans Scholl replied that he had been informed of how relentlessly the Gestapo was after him, and that his informant had told him he would probably be arrested within in few days. In that case, he said, he would have to be active one more time before they rendered him "harmless."

Wilhelm Geyer, the Ulm painter who sometimes worked in Eickemeyer's studio, met the Scholls late on February 16. He too felt a change in both of them. Several times Hans mentioned the time "afterward." Sophie said, "With

163

all those people dying for the regime, it is high time that someone died against it."

So it seems that the Scholls had been warned by someone connected with the Gestapo. And their composure when the janitor pounced on them seems to indicate that they knew the danger they were in. One last warning was supposed to have been given them the very morning of February 18. Inge recalls the episode.

During the first part of February we—Otl Aicher and I—stayed in Munich a few days. We meant to see Hans and Sophie, but it didn't work out. I had to return to my parents in Ulm, while Otl stayed on a few more days as Professor Muth's guest. Hans Hirzel came to see me in our Ulm apartment and asked me to get in touch with Hans immediately and to tell him that the book *Power State and Utopia* was out of print. Now I'm not quite sure. Did I rush immediately to Wilhelm Geyer's place to ask him to pass on the message? At any rate we didn't reach him. So we telephoned Otl Aicher and asked him to see Hans at once.

Otl Aicher completes the story.

Toward the middle of January I was in a military hospital in Linz, Austria, with jaundice which I caught in Russia. Sophie Scholl came to visit me for a few days. No matter how often we discussed politics, she never dropped

164

the slightest hint that she and Hans were behind the activities that preoccupied us so intensely.

I promised her I would come to Munich for a few days as soon as I was released from the hospital. Toward the middle of February I went to Munich, stayed in Professor Muth's house, and before I had a chance to get in touch with Hans and Sophie, I got a phone call from Ulm. I was to inform Hans that the book *Power State and Utopia* was out of print. I called Hans and said I had an important message for him. We made a date for next morning, eleven o'clock, at his apartment, 13 Franz-Joseph-Strasse.

When I got there at eleven, I found the apartment locked. Half an hour later I returned—and was received by the Gestapo. I was searched, and then for about an hour I witnessed the Gestapo search the apartment. They took me, and everything they found relevant, to their car. We were driven to the Wittelsbach Palais. I did not see anything suggesting that Hans and Sophie had produced leaflets. Neither ink nor a mimeograph machine was among the objects seized. As a soldier, I insisted on being transferred to military jurisdiction and was indeed released the next day. I heard about the activities at the university for the first time at Professor Muth's. During my interrogation at Gestapo headquarters I caught sight of Hans for a moment. He seemed so determined and firm that it didn't even occur to me that Hans might be involved in antiregime activities.

165

All That Night the Light Was Kept On

The interrogation in the infamous Wittelsbach Palais took four days. When all their denials became useless, Sophie and Hans took full responsibility for the leaflets and other activities. By doing so, they meant to exculpate their friends. Even the Gestapo officers could not help being impressed by their resolve and the strength of their conviction. After the war one of them, Robert Mohr, reported on the interrogation.

Until the bitter end, Sophie and Hans Scholl maintained a bearing that must be called unique. Both made the same deposition, saying in effect that their activities had had only one purpose: preventing an even greater calamity from overtaking Germany and, if possible, helping to save the lives of hundreds of thousands of German soldiers and people. For, they declared, when the good fortune or misfortune of a great nation was at stake, no expedient and no sacrifice was too great to be offered gladly. Till the very end, Sophie and Hans Scholl were convinced that their sacrifice was not in vain.

There is another testimony from those days, February 18 to 22, 1943, stamped with sympathy and shared suf-

166

fering and therefore more personal and more substantial. A cellmate of Sophie Scholl, Else Gebel, wrote it down after the war and titled it: "In Remembrance of Sophie Scholl." Here are some excerpts from it:

I am looking at a photograph, Sophie—a picture of your brother, Christoph Probst, and you—grave, inquisitive, as if you had a premonition of the cruel fate that would unite the three of you in death.

February 1943. As a political prisoner held in the Munich Gestapo center, I worked in the reception department of the Prison Administration. My job was to register other unfortunates who had fallen into Gestapo hands, and to enter them into the ever-growing card file. For days there had been feverish excitement among the Gestapo men. More and more slogans like DOWN WITH HITLER!, LONG LIVE FREEDOM!, or simply FREEDOM! were being painted on buildings. At the university leaflets had been found scattered in hallways and on stairs at regular intervals, calling on the students to resist. In the Prison Administration we could distinctly feel the air crackling with suspense. None of the investigators came from headquarters, because most of them were assigned to the "Special Search Action." . . .

Thursday the 18th. Early in the morning, headquarters ordered by telephone, "Keep some cells free for the day!" I asked the officer I was assigned to who might be coming, and he answered, "The painters." A few hours later you, Sophie, were standing in the reception room, accompanied by an officer. Calm, serene, almost cheerful about all the excitement surrounding you. Your brother Hans had been booked before and was by now in a cell. Every newcomer had to hand over his papers and belongings and then undergo a body search. The Gestapo had no prison matrons, so I was to do that job. For the first time we faced each other alone, and I had a chance to whisper, "If you have any leaflet with you, destroy it now. I am an inmate myself."

Did you believe me? Or did you think it was a Gestapo trap? I could not tell by your calm, friendly manner. You were not in the least upset. I felt a great sense of relief: They must be thoroughly mistaken. This dear girl with her open, childlike face could never have taken part in such daring activities. You were even put into an "honor cell," mostly reserved for Nazi V.I.P.s gone astray. "Honor" meant that the cell had a wider window, a small cabinet, and white covers for the blankets.

Meanwhile, under guard, I had to get my belongings from my cell and transfer to yours, Sophie. For a short while we were alone again. You were lying on the bed and asked me how long I had been in jail and how I was doing there. And you also told me that you probably were a hard case and could not expect anything good. My advice was that you should under no circumstances con-

168

fess to anything they couldn't prove. "Yes, that's what I have been doing so far, at the university and at a brief Gestapo questioning," you replied, "but there are quite a few things they might find." Then we heard footsteps approaching. You were called for interrogation and I to my job.

Around three o'clock, several male and female students had been brought in. Some were released after a brief questioning. Your brother Hans was being interrogated. What incriminating evidence could those "upstairs" have possibly discovered meanwhile? At six o'clock, dinner was being given out, and the two of you were taken separately to the Prison Administration. A trusty brought you hot soup and bread. Then a telephone call came—"No food for the two Scholls. Their interrogation will continue in thirty minutes." No one downstairs would have even thought of depriving you of your dinner. So at least you both had some sustenance before the interrogation.

At eight o'clock I was through with my last task, listing occupied prison cells. More unfortunates were added to this house of suffering. At ten I went to bed and waited for your return. Sleepless, my heart full of dread, I gazed out into the starry night. To calm myself, I tried to pray for you. The officers had been whispering mysteriously all evening. That rarely boded anything good. Hours and hours passed, and you were not back. In the early morn-

170

ing, tired out, I fell asleep. At 6:30 a trusty brought the coffee—always an opportunity to get whatever news there was. My faint hope that you might have been released during the night was dashed at once. Both of you, I learned, had been interrogated all through the night. Early in the morning, under the impact of incriminating evidence, after hours of denying everything, you had made a confession.

Completely disheartened, I resumed my desolate work. I was afraid of the condition you would be in, so I could hardly believe my eyes when you came back at eight, a bit worse for wear, but completely calm. Standing beside me in the reception room, you got your breakfast and told me that during the night's interrogation you had even got genuine coffee-bean coffee, instead of the artificial stuff everyone was now drinking. When they took you back to the cell, I came along, pretending I had forgotten something. Before my superior sent for me, I did learn a bit of what had happened.

For a long time, Sophie, you had tried to deny everything. But in the university building they had found on Hans the draft of a leaflet. He had torn it up at once and declared that he got it from a student whose name he didn't know. But by that time the Gestapo informers had thoroughly searched your room. The torn-up leaflet was neatly pasted together. The handwriting was that of a friend of yours. You knew that both of you were beyond help. There was only one thing left to do: claim all guilt

171

for yourselves so that no other friend would be endangered.

For a few hours they left you alone. You slept deeply. How I admired you! All those hours of interrogation had done nothing to your calm, relaxed manner. Your unshakable, deep faith gave you strength to sacrifice yourself for others.

Friday night. All through the afternoon you had undergone that questioning and answering, but you were not exhausted at all. You told me that without any doubt, within eight weeks at the most, the Allies' invasion would begin. Then there would be strike after strike, and we would at last be free from this tyranny. How happy I would have been to believe that. But should you, of all people, not be here to see that day? You doubted that you would be. I told you that my brother had been in jail for over a year without trial, and that they would surely take a long time for you two. You sounded more hopeful then. Win time, win all.

That night you told me how often you had distributed the leaflets at the university. In spite of the grave situation, we both laughed when you told me how, recently, on returning from your "scattering tour," you saw a cleaning woman picking up leaflets on the stairs. You walked up to her and said, "Why pick up the leaflets? Just leave them there. The students are supposed to read them." You also mentioned how much aware you people were

172

of the danger: "If ever the Gestapo goons catch us, we pay with our lives." How well I understand your outright exuberance after a night job that had been safely completed—banners hung, or after posting a batch of White Rose letters in outgoing mailboxes. And how you would toast the happy outcome whenever you happened to get a bottle of wine.

You also described your last joint action. After you and Hans had scattered most of the leaflets at the university, you were on Ludwigstrasse with your valise, and you both felt that you really should go home with an empty case. On the spur of the moment you did an about-face, went back into the university, all the way up to the top floor, and with a flourish flung the rest of them into the courtyard. Of course a great commotion followed. The Gestapo had all the doors locked. Everybody had to present an exact ID. Suddenly all hallways were empty. As you went downstairs, Janitor Schmid came toward you to deliver you to the Gestapo. We kept talking and talking that night. Even after we retired I couldn't fall asleep. But I heard your breathing, deep and even.

Saturday morning you were interrogated again for many hours. When I came at noon to give you the glad tidings that now they would definitely leave you alone until Monday morning, you weren't happy at all. You felt the interrogation was provocative and interesting. At least you were lucky in having one of the more or less likable investigators. He, Mohr, had given you a longish lecture on the meaning of National Socialism, the Führer principle, German honor, and how badly you people had undermined Germany's defensive force. Perhaps he meant to give you another chance when he asked, "Miss Scholl, if you had considered all this, you wouldn't have allowed yourself to be carried away with activities of that kind, now would you?" And what did you reply, brave, honest girl that you are? "You are wrong. I would do everything again, exactly the same way. For it is not I who have the wrong philosophy of life, it is you."

That Saturday and Sunday trusties served us our meals. We had a chance to brew tea and coffee, with each of us contributing her bit. In our small cell we had the rarest riches: cigarettes, cookies, sausage, and butter. We even were able to send some of it up to your brother, about whom you were deeply worried. We sent a cigarette inscribed "Freedom" to Willi Graf.

Sunday morning brought you another great shock. The person bringing our morning coffee whispered to me, "Last night another main accomplice was brought in." I told you, and you thought it could only be Alexander Schmorell. By ten a.m., when they called me to my registration job, the recent arrivals had already been registered. I pulled out the index card and read: Christoph Probst, high treason. For two hours I was happy, expecting to tell you that it wasn't Alex who had been caught. But there was horror on your face when I named Christl.

For the first time I saw you uncontrollably shaken. Christl, your good, true friend, father of three small children, whom you had not involved in your activities for the sake of his family, had been dragged into the maelstrom with you because of that draft leaflet! But then you became calm. At the most, Christl would get a prison sentence, which, after all, would not last long.

At noon Mohr came by. He brought fruits, cookies, and a few cigarettes and asked me how you were. He must have felt pity, for he knew better than anyone else what black clouds loomed over you and your friends. Around three o'clock in the afternoon we were sitting together in our cell when you were summoned to receive your bill of indictment. I was told that all three of you would go on trial the very next day. The dreaded "People's Court," the *Volksgerichtshof*, was sitting in Munich; you were going to be doomed by Freisler and his brutal henchmen.

My dearest, dearest Sophie, your fate had been decided. You came back a few minutes later, pale, tremulous. Your hand shook as you started reading the voluminous bill of indictment. But as you read, your face became calmer. By the time you finished, your agitation was gone. "Thank God!" was all you said. Then you asked if I could read the bill without getting into trouble. Even at that hour you didn't want anyone to risk trouble on your behalf. Dear, pure soul, how fond I grew of you in those few days!

Outside, a sunny springlike day. Happy, cheerful people were passing by these walls, not suspecting that here, once again, three courageous, honest young Germans were to be delivered unto death. We lay down on our bunks. In a soft, calm voice you reflected, "Such a glorious, sunny day, and I must go. But how many must die on the battlefields, how many promising young men. . . . What will my death matter if because of our actions thousands of people will be awakened and stirred to action! Surely there will be a revolt among the students." Oh Sophie, you had not learned yet how cowardly is man, the herd animal! "Why, I might just as well die of a disease," you said, "but would that mean the same thing?" I tried again to convince you that you could easily get away with a long prison sentence. But, being a loyal sister, you didn't want to hear of it. "If my brother is sentenced to death, I must not get a lighter sentence, and I don't want to. I am as guilty as he is." You gave the same argument to the court-appointed defense attorney who had been summoned pro forma. He asked if you had a wish—as if such a puppet could get a wish fulfilled for you! No. You only wanted him to confirm that your brother was entitled to death by firing squad, since he was a war veteran. The lawyer had no precise answer. Your further inquiry, whether you yourself would be hanged in public or die under the guillotine, shocked him. Questions like that, asked so calmly, and by a young girl at that—he certainly hadn't expected such a thing. Where strong, war-hardened men tremble, you remained calm and composed. But of course his answers were evasive.

Mohr came by once more and suggested that you write to your family that same day, since in Stadelheim they would probably allow only short notes. Did he mean well? Or did they hope to discover new incriminating information through your letters? Anyway, your family never saw one single line of what you wrote them. At ten o'clock we went to bed. For a while you spoke of your parents and brothers and sisters. The thought of your mother distressed you terribly. To lose two children at the same time! And another son stationed in Russia somewhere! "Father will understand better what we were doing." All that night the light was kept on, and every half hour an officer looked in to make sure that everything was all right. How these people lacked any understanding of your deep piety, your trust in God! For me the night was endless, while you, as before, were fast asleep.

Shortly before seven I had to wake you for this cruel day. You were wide awake at once and told me, sitting up in bed, the dream you had had. It was a fine, sunny day, and you were carrying a baby in a long, white gown to be baptized. The road to the church went up a steep mountainside, but you were holding the baby firmly and safely. Then, without warning, a glacier crevasse suddenly opened. You just barely had time to lay the baby down on the safe side before you plunged down into the

177

abyss. This is how you interpreted the dream: The child in the white gown is our idea. It will prevail against all obstacles. We were allowed to prepare the way of the idea, but first we must die—die for it.

Soon I would be summoned to my job. I believe you could feel how strong my hope for you was, and how my thoughts would constantly be with you. That morning I promised you that in calmer days I would tell your parents of our time together. We shook hands one last time. "May God be with you, Sophie," and I was called away.

Shortly after nine a.m. you were taken to the court-house in a private car, accompanied by two officers. One last glimpse catches my eye—your brother Hans and Christoph Probst, each in handcuffs, are also taken away, separately from you. . . .

Freisler, the Hanging Judge
Or, "These Martyrs Refused
to Humble Themselves"

On Friday, February 19, the elder Scholls learned that their children had been arrested—first from Traute Lafrenz, then from Otl Aicher, who, released by the Gestapo, had returned to Ulm. Then Jürgen Wittenstein called them, probably on Sunday. In addition to the arrest, he had ghastly news: Immediately, this Monday, a trial had been scheduled before the People's Court in Munich.

An anxious weekend passed. Monday morning the parents left for Munich, accompanied by their youngest son, Werner, who had come from Russia on home leave two days before. Jürgen Wittenstein met them at the railway station. He reported that the trial had already started and that they must all be prepared for the worst. They hurried to the courthouse. The People's Court was sitting in Room 216, the infamous Judge Roland Freisler presiding. Freisler had been sent by a special plane from Berlin just for this trial. Proceedings started at 9 a.m. and ended at 2 p.m. Only persons with special passes were admitted—mostly high-ranking party members, who saw the invitation as a mark of distinction. The Scholl parents, though they didn't have passes, managed to get admitted. As it happened, there was another witness to these "judiciary proceedings" staged by Freisler, a Dr. Leo Samberger, a future attorney but at the time still a junior lawyer. In February 1968 he wrote a report on this episode, in which he says:

Either by accident or by providence—for the proceedings had started earlier, about 9 a.m.—I was told at my cigarette dealer's near the courthouse that at that moment some students were in court for their seditious activities.

I went there immediately. It was about 10:30, and the trial was in full swing. I stayed near the entrance. The courtroom was crowded, tense faces everywhere. My first impression was that most of them were ashen with fear, fear emanating from the judge's bench. Possibly there were some shaken-up Party-believers, or possibly stool pigeons, whose pallor would be due to different feelings.

Then I concentrated on the main action, the trial proceedings. After a quarter-century, from an enormous mass of impressions, there are still some isolated, striking images which impressed themselves like symbols on my memory. Above all the infamous Presiding Judge of the People's Court, Roland Freisler: raging, screaming, roar-

180

ing till his voice broke, jumping up again and again in red-hot explosions. He had been considered a competent lawyer until he revealed his true colors. His coarse face with its pop eyes and fleshy ears sticking out contrasted strangely with the dignified beret on his head. It seemed that in all these proceedings his purpose was to generate lasting, widespread terror and dread, and to suppress the feelings of all those who felt that the defendants' courageous act was admirable and magnificent.

I personally was deeply affected when I discovered that, though I did not know the defendants, I knew their faces quite well. I had often seen them in Munich concert halls. During those years, many people sought strength and refuge in Haydn's, Mozart's, and Beethoven's music.

Surely I was not the only one whom the defendants' attitude impressed deeply. These people were visibly and truly devoted to their ideals. The presiding judge, who acted more like a prosecutor than a judge throughout the trial, asked many insolent questions. The answers were calm, composed, clear, and unflinching.

Only their physical reactions revealed the extreme tension they had to withstand. Hans Scholl, standing straight, suddenly turned white, as if he were fainting, and shook all over. He threw his head back and closed his eyes, but he did not fall. He answered the next question in a firm voice. His sister Sophie and his friend Christoph

Probst, who was partly hidden from the audience, displayed the same steadfast attitude.

Freisler's revolting purpose was to show the defendants up, again and again, as a combination of simpletons and criminals, even though their appearance must have made that somewhat difficult for him. At one point, in a discussion about paper supplies, he even mentioned theft. He just had to destroy any suspicion that these were honorable people acting for the great goal of arousing the nation to duty and freedom. But these martyrs, in the last hours of their lives, refused to humble themselves.

After this interrogation—which put the law to shame for a long time—after these hypocritical and insulting proceedings, the plea of the National Prosecutor, who, as expected, demanded the death penalty, sounded businesslike and relatively bland. The court-appointed defense attorneys said a few words, revealing no true endeavor to serve the people they were representing. Hans Scholl's attorney, for instance, protested that no one could possibly understand why people would do such things, things one ought to be ashamed of.

After this inferior defense, a middle-aged man, very agitated, pushed through the audience to the front of the courtroom. He tried to get the floor, first through the defense attorney and, when this failed, on his own. He was Hans and Sophie Scholl's father, present in the courtroom though definitely uninvited by Gestapo and court, making one last, desperate effort to suggest to the court ideas in favor of the defendants, his children. He tried desperately to be heard a few more times. When Freisler realized what was going on, he made short shrift of the annoyance, ordered the parents to leave the courtroom (it turned out that the mother was there too), and had them ushered out.

Around 1:30 the judge withdrew to deliberate. During the recess, the loathsome university janitor, dressed in his Sunday best to watch his great show, had himself admired and celebrated as a neglected hero.

After the judge's brief deliberation, the crowds returned to the courtroom. Nobody wanted to miss the sensational sentencing. There were only two people left in the wide hall outside the courtroom: the parents of Hans and Sophie Scholl, banished from the courtroom. My indignation had reached its full measure, so had my sympathy for them. While the doors were being closed, I walked out and approached the parents. I introduced myself as a fledgling lawyer, told them in a few words how the proceedings had nauseated me, and offered them my help in this desperate situation, knowing full well that all that was left would be human help. While the sentence was pronounced in the courtroom, we discussed the proceedings.

Presently the doors opened; the audience came out;

183

the sentence we had expected was confirmed. Outwardly, the parents showed admirable composure. The father tried, though, to vent his horror through loud words. I urged him to stay calm lest he worsen the catastrophe. Hans Scholl's court-appointed defense lawyer approached the parents without one word of regret, one gesture of sympathy. He had the nerve to blame the parents for the actions of their children.

Mr. Scholl asked me if there was anything that could be done, and I suggested that we go immediately to the Attorney General to file a petition for clemency. The secretary took down our application in the anteroom. It was with great difficulty that we managed to get an interview for Mr. Scholl with the Attorney General, who passed on our request for an audience with the National Prosecutor himself—but to no avail. I said good-bye and gave Mr. Scholl my telephone number and address, asking him to call me at once if I could be of any help.

"That Will Fan the Flames"

At the end of the five-hour-long proceedings, Freisler pronouced the sentence: death by guillotine. The defendants were given a chance to say a last word. Sophie Scholl kept silent. Christl Probst pleaded for his life, for the sake of his children. Hans Scholl tried to back up his friend's plea, but Freisler cut him short: "If you have nothing to advance in your own behalf, be good enough to shut up." Then the three were taken to the Execution Prison in Stadelheim, a Munich suburb right next to the Perlach cemetery. They wrote their farewell letters. There was a last meeting, probably by accident, of Hans and Sophie with their parents. Inge Scholl reports on this in her book, *The White Rose*.

My parents had the miraculous good fortune of being able to visit their children one last time. It was almost impossible to obtain such permission. They hurried to the prison between four and five p.m. They still did not know that their children's last hour was so near.

Hans was led in first. He wore a prison uniform, but he walked upright and briskly. The circumstances could not detract from his inner essence. His face was thin and drawn, as if after a hard struggle. But it was radiant and outshone everything else. He bent lovingly over the bar that separated him from them and shook their hands. "I have no hatred. I have put everything, everything behind me." My father embraced him and said, "You both will be enshrined in history, there is still such a thing as justice." Then Hans asked them to remember him to his friends. As he mentioned one last name, a tear ran down his face, and he bent down over the bar to hide it. And then he turned and left, without the slightest fear, borne by a deep, glorious enthusiasm.

Then Sophie was brought in by a woman warden. She wore her own clothes and walked slowly and easily and very upright. (Nowhere do you learn to walk as upright as in prison.) She kept smiling as if she were looking into the sun. Gladly and cheerfully she accepted the candy Hans had refused. "Oh yes, of course. Why, I haven't had any lunch yet." It was an indescribable affirmation of life right up to the end, to the very last moment. She too was a shade thinner, but her face radiated a miraculous triumph. Her complexion was rosy and fresh. Her mother was struck by that as never before. Her lips were a glowing deep red. "So now we will never see you walk in through the door again," said Mother. "Oh Mother those few short years!" she replied. Then she insisted, like her brother, firmly, in triumphant conviction, "We took all responsiblity, for everything." And she added, "That will fan the flames."

186

Her great worry all through those days had been one question: How would her mother bear the ordeal of losing two children at the same time? But as Mother stood there, so unflinching and good, Sophie had a feeling of relief, almost of deliverance. Again Mother spoke. She meant to give her daughter something she might hold fast to. "Remember, Sophie: Jesus." Gravely, firmly, almost imperiously Sophie replied, "Yes—but you must remember too." Then she too left—free, fearless, serene.

"She Went Without Batting an Eyelash"

The prison wardens, astonished and thunderstruck by the strength of these three condemned people, did them one favor. Before dying, the three were allowed to be together for a few moments. The warden's report reads:

They were so incredibly brave. The entire prison was impressed. That was why we took the risk—had we been found out, there would have been grave consequences—of bringing the three of them together, right before the execution. We wanted them to be able to smoke one last cigarette together. It was only a few minutes, but I believe it meant a great deal to them. "I didn't know that dying could be so easy," said Christl Probst. "In a few minutes we meet again in eternity."

Then they were led away, first the girl. She went without batting an eyelash. None of us could understand how such a thing was possible. The executioner said he had never seen anyone die like that.

And Hans, before he put his head on the block, cried in a loud voice—you could hear it reverberate throughout the large prison—"Long live freedom!"

On February 23, 1943, the newspaper *Münchener Neueste Nachrichten* carried this death notice:

Death Sentences for Conspiracy to Commit High Treason. The People's Court, on February 22, 1943, in the assizes courtroom of the courthouse, sentenced Hans Scholl, 24, Sophie Scholl, 21, both of Munich, and Christoph Probst, 23, of Aldrans near Innsbruck, to death and to loss of rights and privileges of citizenship for conspiring to commit high treason and for aiding and abetting the enemy. The sentence was carried out the same day. The culprits, typical loners, had transgressed shamelessly against the defensive strength and the spirit of the German nation by smearing house walls with subversive incitements and by disseminating fliers fomenting high treason. In view of the heroic fight of the German nation, depraved elements of that kind have earned nothing but quick and dishonorable death.

During the following months about eighty persons were arrested and sentenced in Munich and other southern and western German cities. Professor Kurt Huber, Willi Graf, and Alexander Schmorell were sentenced to death on April 19 [and executed a few months later]. Traute Lafrenz, Katharina Schüddekopf, Gisela Schertling, and Susanne Hirzel each were sentenced to one year in prison, Hans Hirzel to five years, Eugen Grimminger to life in prison. In a third trial, on July 13, 1943, Josef Soehngen, Wilhelm Geyer, and Manfred Eickemeyer were given three months in prison.

With that, the White Rose had been crushed. Its Hamburg branch was discovered also. Some fifty people were arrested; eight of them went to their deaths.

189

To Survive;
To Go On Living

"You Cannot Live Without Hope" (Ilse Aichinger)

A Radio News Item

On the night of that terrible day, the day of the death sentence and execution, Leo Samberger, the young lawyer, had another horrible ordeal: facing the parents of Hans and Sophie. Robert Scholl had called him and asked to see him. Leo Samberger recalls:

We made an appointment and met around 6:30 in the Humpelmayr tavern. Besides the parents there was a younger brother, who happened to be home on leave from the front, and a woman student who had been close to the circle and a friend of Hans Scholl's. She was to go on trial herself soon.

Mr. Scholl asked me to write the appeal for clemency on behalf of the co-defendant, Christoph Probst, at once. It was to be taken the next morning to Christoph Probst's wife, who was in childbed in Tegernsee, to be signed by her and then immediately submitted to the authorities.

After I handed the appeal to Mr. Scholl, an aquaintance of mine, who happened to be sitting at a nearby table, told me that it had been announced on the radio that the death sentences had been carried out at 5 p.m. that evening. I could not bring myself to tell the family. We spent a few hours talking about the terrible day. I also tried to get them to calm down. Around ten o'clock we took the parents to their train to Ulm. Afterwards I took a short walk with the brother [who later died in Russia], in the quiet streets of nighttime Munich. Then we went our separate ways.

"They Are Dead"

The Scholls returned to Ulm in the belief that their children would not be executed right away and were still alive. They told their daughter Inge about the trial and asked her to take the next train to Munich. Perhaps there would be a chance for her to see Hans and Sophie. Inge reports:

The next morning I took the first train to Munich. Otl Aicher came with me. Werner had remained in Munich. First we went to the Attorney General's office to get a visitor's permit. How well I remember that day, a radiant spring day. The Attorney General was not there. His secretary received us. She came up to me, took both my hands in hers and said, "They are dead. Both were so indescribably brave dying. Now you too will have to be brave."

We left and tended to some things, I don't recall what—we just walked the Munich streets until we finally came to the building where Hans and Sophie lived. I went into Sophie's room. On her desk there was a plant. Its pale-lavender petals reminded me of fluttering butterflies. She had mentioned the flower in a letter to Fritz Hartnagel. I sat down at the desk and found Sophie's diary, overlooked by the Gestapo in their search. A gift of Heaven, I felt.

On February 24 Sophie and Hans Scholl were buried in the Perlach cemetery, right next to the Stadelheim prison where they had been executed. Inge recalls:

We were allowed to bury them, which had been far from a certainty, but the system still tried to hold on to middle-class appearances.

The burial took place in the late afternoon. The sun had almost set when we left the cemetery—in deep silence. After a time my mother said that it was time to think about dinner. She implied something like: I have to take care of the living children as well. We all—Traute Lafrenz had come too—went to a restaurant. Mother lumped together the food ration cards covering who knows how many days' and weeks' worth of meat rations and ordered a hefty meal. And I kept thinking: That was the way Sophie would have liked her to act. That imperious "command" of Sophie's in the execution prison—"But you must remember too, Mother"—that affirmation of life prevailed even in the cruelest hours. So later on I tried to build within my modest scope from experiences and sacrifices something that can show man a path into the future, that will help him, stimulate him, enrich him.

196

"Kinship Detention" for the Rest of the Family

Not content with the execution of Sophie and Hans Scholl, holding an offender's family liable for his misdeeds, the National Socialists announced "kinship detention" (Sippenhaft) for the rest of the Scholl family. There was nothing to charge them with at first, but those grounds would be easy to find. Inge tells of the days after her brother's and sister's burials:

We returned to Ulm from Munich the evening of that day: my parents, my brother Werner, Elisabeth, and I. We were sitting together in deep exhaustion, strangely adrift, and suddenly I said to my father, "I think we have to be prepared for more. At the very least they will not let you continue working."

Three days later we were having breakfast together when the doorbell rang. The Gestapo had come to pick us up. Only Werner was allowed to remain. He was in uniform, hence under army jurisdiction. By now we knew one of the officers quite well from our father's and our own arrests. He insisted again and again that he didn't know what was going to happen to us but that for the time being he would have to take us into "protective custody." He kept interrogating us, along with the Munich Gestapo. He swore to high heaven that he couldn't tell what was wrong with us. We really belonged in a concentration camp, he said, almost good-naturedly. Of course we were glad to be allowed to stay in prison—[anything but concentration camp!].

A few days later Werner had to return to the eastern front so could no longer visit us. But another soldier did: Fritz Hartnagel, Sophie's friend, who had had a narrow escape from the murderous battle of Stalingrad. He was alive, though pale and drained, his hands in bandages. He visited us as often as he could. Everybody respected a Stalingrad soldier.

Easter 1943 came. Once in a while we received news about the military situation and about the arrests of the other White Rose members. We learned that Professor Kurt Huber, Alexander Schmorell, and Willi Graf had also been sentenced to death. Pentecost came, and we still were not free. Only my sister Elisabeth had been released, because of kidney trouble. She roamed all over Ulm trying to find a lawyer for us. Her life outside prison walls was almost grimmer than ours. She had to live with other people's fears—she saw the panic she provoked by greeting an acquaintance. Most of them looked away as if they were afraid of being contaminated. Elisabeth sometimes felt like a leper.

Eventually they discovered evidence to incriminate the three of us. Allegedly someone had reported—probably their own invention—that we had listened to Thomas Mann on a Swiss radio station. We secretly grinned. Of course we had heard Thomas Mann, but on BBC, the British station. They interrogated us about that charge, and my mother and I were put in solitary. In the following weeks I contracted a kind of diphtheria, and my mother's health grew worse every day. The court authorities released my mother and me temporarily for reasons of health late in July.

Our trial was in August and it was on that occasion we saw my father. Calm, yet resigned, we expected a prison sentence. To our surprise, the judge acquitted my mother and me. My father got two years of hard labor. The saddest moment for the two of us, the free ones, was going back from the courthouse into our beautiful apartment on cathedral plaza, leaving my father in his bleak cell.

After 1945 Inge Scholl founded the Ulm University for Adult Education because she was convinced that "unless its citizens possess a sound foundation of knowledge, democracy will stand on shaky feet." For twelve long years, a propaganda apparatus that controlled everything, along with a surveillance apparatus that paralyzed everything, had isolated Germany from the outside world and from the minds that were developing there. Starting from scratch

199

opened up new opportunities. "It gave us a great chance," said Inge, "and a challenge to get busy in a program of modernized adult education."

As a complement to adult education, Inge Scholl, together with Otl Aicher and a group of friends, prepared the foundation for an Academy of Design, which finally got started in Ulm in October 1955. It was to train young people in designing their cultural environment. Several different fields were to be covered: appliances and utensils, the home, the city, the landscape, mass media. Modern, open-minded teaching created an atmosphere where intellectual and manual principles could be attuned to each other. After ten years, however, the Ulm Academy of Design was closed—because of absurd politics, says Inge Aicher-Scholl. The University for Adult Education continues. Its founder feels it promises further hopeful development "provided the bureaucracy won't choke it to death."

"I was Stunned"
After Stalingrad, the Message from Ulm

It was much later that Fritz Hartnagel learned of his friend's death. The last time he had seen her was in May of 1942. He had had to return to Russia, and the only link between them was their letters. The scouting company he headed took part in the Sixth Army's drive on Stalingrad and it was surrounded along with that army. He was wounded and, almost miraculously, escaped the Stalingrad hell on one of the last planes. A letter from Mrs. Scholl reached him in a Polish military hospital. Fritz Hartnagel recalls:

She told me that a trial against Sophie and Hans had been held at the People's Court and that they both had been sentenced to death. When she wrote this letter, she obviously did not know yet that the sentences had been carried out. I reported to the Chief Surgeon, who showed understanding for my situation and granted me leave to go to Ulm. On the way I stopped in Berlin in order to submit a petition for clemency to the People's Court, but the evening before that I telephoned Ulm from Berlin. Sophie's brother Werner was the only one at home. It was from him that I learned that Sophie and Hans had been executed and that thereupon their parents and sisters, Inge and Elisabeth, now my wife, had been taken into kinship detention.

At first I was stunned. The news was such a shock. All I could tell Werner was that I would be in Ulm on the next train. I am not a man given to great emotional outbursts, but it was a wretched time for me, and even more so when I arrived in Ulm and no one was there but Werner. With my wound I was not yet fit for armed service. I roamed all over Ulm, alone, deeply depressed. One first ray of relief was when Elisabeth was released from prison late in April for reasons of health. From that moment, a close relationship arose between us quite spontaneously. It was the logical continuation of my relationship with Sophie. I had known the Scholl family for many years. After all these horrible events, it was the most natural thing for us to draw together.

After the war Fritz Hartnagel went to law school and became a judge. He was against the rearmament of the Federal Republic of Germany in the second half of the 1950s, since he thought it would be impossible to rebuild a German army without the old Nazi officers. For many years he counseled conscientious objectors and was active in the fight against atomic armament. In the 1960s he took part in the [war resisters'] Easter Marches and in resistance to the [peremptory] Emergency Powers Act of 1968.

202

"Not Accommodating Oneself . . ."

A Conversation with Ilse Aichinger
about Sophie Scholl

When Inge Scholl tried "to build, out of experiences and sacrifices, something that can show man the path into the future," she was not alone. Others helped her, among them the Austrian writer and lyrical poet Ilse Aichinger, born in 1921 like Sophie Scholl and deeply influenced by the Scholls' fate.

In 1948 she published her first novel, *Die grössere Hoffnung* (English: *Herod's Children,* 1963), the story of a girl racially persecuted by the Hitler regime. Its forgiving mood can be traced to the influence of Hans and Sophie Scholl. In the early 1950s she wrote a long radio play about them. She intimately knows their letters and diaries. She collaborated in the writing of Inge Scholl's book *The White Rose* and, during the same period, in establishing the Academy of Design in Ulm. Soon she began to write stories and radio plays. With her poetry, perched between wide-awake daytime knowledge and dreamlike nighttime experience, she became one of the most important German postwar writers. In 1953 she married the lyrical poet Günter Eich, who died twenty years later. She has maintained a firm friendship with Sophie Scholl's sisters and friends since their time in Ulm.

One February afternoon I visited Ilse Aichinger in the small Austrian town of Grossmain near the German border. Fog banks appeared to separate the surrounding mountains from the earth. Ilse Aichinger is not very fond of those mighty rock walls. They seem threatening to her. But she has remained in the house where she lived with Günter Eich, who died in 1973. Her 88-year-old mother, with whom she shared the terror of the Hitler years, lives with her.

In her peaceful household, the past is as hauntingly present as the surrounding mountains. In 1942, Ilse Aichinger's maternal grandmother was deported to a concentration camp and died there. Ilse Aichinger wrote about her, "Whoever forgets the dead kills them all over again. We must stay on the track of the dead. I have that tie with my grandmother. She has a comforting way of being here. So has Günter." She could have added: So have the Scholl children and their companions. For Ilse Aichinger they are still there, they are still alive. When she speaks of them it is in a highly lyrical, almost biblical language that sometimes conjures up her poetry. Here is Ilse Aichinger, on this February afternoon, 1980.

HERMANN VINKE: Miss Aichinger, you lived in Vienna with your mother in February 1943 when the so-called enemy radio stations, BBC and Swiss stations, broadcast the news that the Scholls and other White Rose members had been executed. Where and how did you get the news?

ILSE AICHINGER: Since I am half-Jewish (my mother is Jewish), we were not allowed to own a radio. Listening to a foreign station on someone else's radio would have been twice as dangerous. On one of those early, precocious spring days we sometimes have in February, I saw the names on a poster on a wall in the inner city near the Jewish temple, near Gestapo headquarters and near [the nineteenth-century poet] Adalbert Stifter's house. It was one of those unmistakable posters pillorying persons sentenced to death. That is where I first saw the names of the members of the White Rose. I did not know any of them, but one thing I can tell you. From those names an incomparable hope flashed over me. And not only me. This hope made it possible for us to go on living in those days, even though it had nothing to do with hope of survival.

HERMANN VINKE: Can you describe what you mean: Did you discuss it with friends?

ILSE AICHINGER: I belonged to some youth groups where these names came to shine like a beacon of hope. They helped many of the dying, helped them to die in hope. They helped others to live—in spite of everything. It was like a secret radiance that spread over the land, like a happiness. I remember meeting an acquaintance on the street one day, and he said to me, "Don't beam so! They'll arrest you for beaming." That is how it was. We didn't have much of a chance to survive, but survival was not what counted. Life counted. Life itself touched our hearts through the death of Hans and Sophie Scholl and their friends.

HERMANN VINKE: Did the fate of this resistance group determine your reaction to what you had to go through, what your family went through?

ILSE AICHINGER: Yes, it helped me a great deal, as it helped my mother, to endure those last, perilous times calmly, almost peacefully. Hope. That was what it gave us. After all, there are so many things you can live without. You can live without having anything. But you cannot live without having something *ahead of you*, and not just a future in time. You have to see a future *within yourself*. You cannot live without hope. And this hope had grown so very strong during the last years, especially after the Scholls and their friends had been executed.

HERMANN VINKE: Did you come to know details about this resistance group at the time?

ILSE AICHINGER: Few at that time. Only after the war did I read the exact story of the White Rose in an English

208

newspaper—as much as an illustrated paper can give a detailed story—and saw the first photographs. That story called me back into the past so intensely that I—you might misunderstand, but it happened—felt a nostalgia for the dark times, and above all for the Scholl children. After I had dropped out of medical school and had written a book, *The Greater Hope,* on that time of persecution, I was very happy when Inge Scholl invited me for the first time to read in Germany. And thus, the Ulm University for Adult Education came to be the first house I entered in Germany, Ulm the first city, and Inge Scholl with her circle of friends, the first people I saw there.

HERMANN VINKE: Miss Aichinger, you have written about the Scholls. How can you explain that one group of young people, loving life, suddenly decided to fight the regime, while at the same time 99 percent of their contemporaries were ready to go to war?

ILSE AICHINGER: Why, war is one way of hiding death from death, of covering up death with death, of avoiding the need to face things, to face life as well as death. After all, [in German] you don't say a soldier has died—you merely say he has fallen. Many, I believe, simply succumbed to war. And of course they were forced.

HERMANN VINKE: What part did home life play in this context?

ILSE AICHINGER: The Scholls' middle-class parental home was important in that it was a place where books had always been read. Literature and politics had been discussed and debated. The Scholls had a politically oriented home. Those are pillars which support independent thought.

HERMANN VINKE: A politically oriented home life, but surely a tolerant one as well.

ILSE AICHINGER: Very tolerant. It simply allowed the children to explore in all directions. They belonged to the youth movement. For a short while they belonged to the Hitler Youth. They were merely warned in the softest of voices. They were let go. So they safely got over that cliff, particularly Sophie Scholl. In her letters and diaries you can see clearly that martyrs are not born accidentally. Had she never been confronted with that destiny, but rather met any other destiny, any seemingly middle-class, seemingly sheltered destiny, she would have been exactly the same person. She would have measured up to the same standard.

HERMANN VINKE: In Sophie Scholl's diaries and letters there is a striking clarity of thought when she discusses war and soldiering. At the same time you are aware of intense feeling, emotion, sympathy. Isn't that a contradiction?

ILSE AICHINGER: Sophie Scholl at one point wrote that you must have a hard spirit and a soft heart. There is no contradiction there. She affirmed life. Never as long as she lived did she believe in what the Nazis bombastically called a hero's death, in solemnities with a drum roll. Never. She believed in life—till the very end, I believe, till her last dream the night before the execution.

HERMANN VINKE: Sophie Scholl had many dreams, and some of them she wrote down. How do they impress you?

ILSE AICHINGER: Why, they are so precise! As precise as one sometimes wishes language could be. When I read Joseph Conrad or James Joyce, I am reminded of the preciseness of Sophie Scholl's dreams, the exactitude that cannot be fooled.

At one point she wrote, "We carry all our standards within ourselves, only we don't look for them closely enough. Perhaps because they are the severest standards." The exactitude of dreams, their precison . . . one could almost say their clairvoyance, but that is such a hackneyed word. Let me say precision.

HERMANN VINKE: Which would mean some reality in the midst of unreality.

ILSE AICHINGER: Yes, some much higher reality than the existing reality, either then or now, could offer us. Existing reality cannot give spontaneously without asking for something in return. It presents itself only when you counteract

211

it, when you refuse to recognize it, when you do not accommodate yourself.

HERMANN VINKE: Did you have a particular dream of hers in mind? Or could you relate what you just said to one of the dreams she described?

ILSE AICHINGER: I think it is the dream she had in her last night, where she was climbing the steep mountain, the baby in her arms, and suddenly the glacier crevasse opened. But, she said, she was able to put the baby on the safe side before she plunged down.

HERMANN VINKE: Sophie Scholl joined the White Rose very soon after she started her Munich University studies in May of 1942. Could it have been because she admired her big brother so much? Or was it an independent decision?

ILSE AICHINGER: Both, I suppose. But at any rate it was a very independent decision. After all, she could easily have said: I won't get involved; I cannot do that to my parents; if you people do that, I'll move out. But in full independence, without regard for all that, she made up her mind to resist. At that moment she must have been well aware of things. When you have been living in Nazi Germany, you are well aware of what the greater likelihood will be.

HERMANN VINKE: I believe that in some respects Sophie

Scholl had even greater resolve than other members of the resistance group. Whence this radicalism, which we sometimes see in women?

ILSE AICHINGER: This radicalism was born with her. I have often wondered, but I am sure that, say on a school excursion, she would have tramped along as all the others did, covered with dust, picking flowers. And no one could really have distinguished her from the others, except perhaps by her happiness and her openness. We cannot know the exact moment when Sophie Scholl made the decision against herself for the first time. But that moment occurred as surely as there is a point in a geometric design from which the lines radiate and upon which they converge. There is a passage she wrote during her labor service. "So far I have been able to keep myself in the background, thanks to my shyness. If only I could go on like that. I am trying very hard to keep myself untouched by the influences of the moment. Not the philosophical and political influences—they certainly don't matter to me any longer, but the moods." And then, you see there's this passage: "You must have a hard spirit and a soft heart."

HERMANN VINKE: There are people who have said, and still say, that what the White Rose did, what those Munich students did fighting National Socialism, was unreasonable and foolhardy.

213

ILSE AICHINGER: "Reason" is a very dangerous word. One must have it. Everybody must have it, but only so that he can throw it overboard at the critical moment. "Foolhardy" is too easily said. Foolhardiness, I don't know . . . They knew exactly what their activities would do to their own lives. And they had an inkling of what their activities would do to the future, even if now it does look as if they were wrong. They sensed that they were starting a gust of wind where all had been becalmed. They sensed it more strongly than we do now. In fact they *knew* it. They gave their lives for others, in nonviolence. That is why I say that the Scholls and their friends, in trying to resist, succeeded, that their resistance carried the day, that perhaps it was the most successful resistance in the Third Reich.

HERMANN VINKE: Was it a political resistance?

ILSE AICHINGER: It was of course a political resistance. But once the line has been crossed, is there anything that is not political? Yet I would say it was more than a political resistance. It arose from Sophie's innermost self. Really it was a resistance of life, of truth, of warmth and most of all of the spirit. I am convinced that what the Scholls and their friends started, what Sophie—especially Sophie, as a girl—started, is still at work. It is still pulsating in the air.

HERMANN VINKE: In 1968 Munich University held a memorial service for the Scholls and their comrades-in-arms. Some student hecklers said: You people have no right to honor them; you people are hypocrites. Who on earth has a right to honor them? Has anybody?

ILSE AICHINGER: To be sure, each of us must first earn this right by fighting for it within his own soul. Who can decide which of the celebrants, in 1968 or today, has that right, and which one has usurped it? You know if you have it; I know if I have it. We cannot speak for anyone else.

But we have to realize that those resisters were never among the conformists. Here is a passage from Sophie Scholl's diary that proves it:

Tonight, as I looked up for a moment from the general jolly merry-making, as I looked out through the window at the evening sky, through the bare trees at the yellow horizon, suddenly I remembered that it was Good Friday. The sky seemed strangely far away and indifferent and it saddened me. Or perhaps it was the people with their empty laughter, for whom the sky had no relevance. I felt excluded from the merry party and from the unconcerned sky.

And here is the passage that I think is decisive:

I fear that I have started getting used to the place. I'll have to summon up my strength. My nightly reading will help me.

I believe she was reading Saint Augustine at the time, but she might just as well have been reading Marx. Her nightly readings did help her.

There is a true story about Gustav Heinemann. On his birthday, a group of young people in Bonn serenaded him. Of course he was one politician who [even as President of the Federal Republic] managed never to pronounce a platitude. He came out and told the young people, in effect: "You are young. Your job is to grow up." Today, whenever I look at children or adolescents, I wonder: How would *you* manage to cope with a death sentence, passed either by the political powers or by physicians? How will *you* manage to grow old?

HERMANN VINKE: What do you think today's young people can learn by becoming involved with the Scholls and the White Rose?

ILSE AICHINGER: Not to accommodate themselves. To forget their petty little dreams so that the great dreams will not be forgotten. To accommodate themselves even less than ever before to this world, which is driving them, more and more strongly into despair, especially young people.